Words, Words, Words

TOPICS IN TRANSLATION

Series Editors: Susan Bassnett (*University of Warwick*)
and André Lefevere (*University of Texas, Austin*)

Editor for Annotated Texts for Translation: Beverly Adab (*Aston University, Birmingham*)

Editor for Translation in the Commercial Environment:
Geoffrey Samuelsson-Brown (*Aardvark Translation Services Ltd*)

Other Books in the Series

Annotated Texts for Translation: French – English
  BEVERLY ADAB
Annotated Texts for Translation: English – French
  BEVERLY ADAB
Linguistic Auditing
  NIGEL REEVES and COLIN WRIGHT
Paragraphs on Translation
  PETER NEWMARK
Practical Guide for Translators
  GEOFFREY SAMUELSSON-BROWN
The Coming Industry of Teletranslation
  MINAKO O'HAGAN
Translation, Power, Subversion
  ROMAN ÁLVAREZ and M. CARMEN-ÁFRICA VIDAL (eds)

Other Books of Interest

About Translation
  PETER NEWMARK
Cultural Functions of Translation
  C. SCHÄFFNER and H. KELLY-HOLMES (eds)

Please contact us for the latest book information:
Multilingual Matters Ltd, Frankfurt Lodge, Clevedon Hall,
Victoria Road, Clevedon, Avon BS21 7SJ, England

TOPICS IN TRANSLATION 7
Series Editors: Susan Bassnett (*University of Warwick*) and
André Lefevere (*University of Texas, Austin*)

Words, Words, Words

The Translator and the Language Learner

Edited by

Gunilla Anderman and Margaret Rogers

> *Polonius*: What do you read, my lord?
> *Hamlet*: Words, words, words
> *Hamlet* Act 2, Scene 2, l. 195

MULTILINGUAL MATTERS LTD
Clevedon • Philadelphia • Adelaide

Library of Congress Cataloging in Publication Data

Words, Words, Words: The Translator and the Language Learner
Edited by Gunilla Anderman and Margaret Rogers
Topics in Translation: 7
Includes bibliographical references and index.
1. Second language acquisition. 2. Translating and interpreting. 3. Vocabulary.
I. Anderman, Gunilla, M. II. Rogers, Margaret, A. III. Series.
P118.2.W87   1996
401'.93–dc20   95-43551

British Library Cataloguing in Publication Data

A CIP catalogue record for this book is available from the British Library.

ISBN 1-85359-332-X (hbk)
ISBN 1-85359-331-1 (pbk)

Multilingual Matters Ltd

UK: Frankfurt Lodge, Clevedon Hall, Victoria Road, Clevedon, Avon BS21 7SJ.
USA: 1900 Frost Road, Suite 101, Bristol, PA 19007, USA.
Australia: P.O. Box 6025, 83 Gilles Street, Adelaide, SA 5000, Australia.

Copyright © 1996 Gunilla Anderman, Margaret Rogers and the authors of individual chapters.

All rights reserved. No part of this work may be reproduced in any form or by any means without permission in writing from the publisher.

Typeset by Archetype, Stow-on-the-Wold.
Index compiled by Meg Davies (Society of Indexers)

Contents

Contributors: A Short Profile vi

Preface vii

1   The Translator and the Language Learner: Linguistics Revisited
    Gunilla Anderman and Margaret Rogers 1

2   Taming the Wilderness: Words in the Mental Lexicon
    Jean Aitchison 15

3   The Classical Research in L2 Vocabulary Acquisition
    Paul Meara 27

4   The Word is My Oyster: The Language Learner and the Translator
    Gunilla Anderman 41

5   Looking at English Words in Translation
    Peter Newmark 56

6   Lexical Innovation: Neologism and Dictionaries
    John Ayto 63

7   Beyond the Dictionary: The Translator, the L2 Learner and
    the Computer
    Margaret Rogers 69

Index 96

Contributors: A Short Profile

Jean Aitchison is Rupert Murdoch Professor of Language Communication, Worcester College, University of Oxford.

Gunilla Anderman is the Director of the Programme in Translation Studies, University of Surrey and teaches Translation Theory on the Diploma/MA in Translation.

John Ayto is a freelance lexicographer. He also teaches on the Postgraduate Diploma/MA in Translation at the University of Surrey.

Dr Paul Meara is the Director of the Centre for Applied Language Studies, University College, Swansea.

Professor Peter Newmark teaches Principles and Methods of Translation on the Postgraduate Diploma/MA in Translation at the University of Surrey.

Margaret Rogers is the Deputy Director of the Programme in Translation Studies, University of Surrey and teaches Text Analysis and Terminology on the Diploma/MA in Translation.

Preface

During the late 1980s and early 1990s a number of linguists engaged in research into different aspects of the lexicon were the guests of the Programme in Translation Studies in the Department of Linguistic and International Studies at the University of Surrey. The present volume contains some of the papers which resulted from this co-operation, together with contributions from colleagues with a particular interest in first and second language acquisition and/or translation. It was felt that, given the recent interest in different aspects of vocabulary studies, the papers would provide a potentially fruitful combination, linking ideas from different but, as it turns out, related fields. It was also felt that whereas translation studies had already tried to draw on the findings from a number of different disciplines, observations from the fields of first and second language acquisition had not, so far, been specifically related to translation.

The study of vocabulary may, of course, be approached from many different angles. In the present volume, the reader interested in learning about vocabulary is invited to share some of the recent research findings about words in a number of different areas — how we learn them, store them, retrieve them in our first and second languages, how they are included in dictionaries and, finally, how we translate them. It is intended for those interested in reading around the subject of vocabulary, such as language teachers, students on advanced language courses, teachers of translation, postgraduate students on academic translation programmes, translators and, in addition, anyone interested in words, words, words...

1 The Translator and the Language Learner — Linguistics Revisited

GUNILLA ANDERMAN AND MARGARET ROGERS

Translation Studies and Linguistics

In considering the nature of translation studies as a relatively new discipline, it would seem only natural to view its emergence in the broader context of developments in the study of language. It is hardly surprising, therefore, to find that in the 1950s–1960s, at the time when Noam Chomsky put forward his ideas about a theory-based approach to the description of natural language, attempts were also made to develop a similar framework for the study of translation. In the United States, the writings of Eugene Nida reflected, as might be expected, the approach of American linguists at the time. Nida adapted Chomsky's grammatical model, then known as Transformational Generative Grammar, and analysed complex constructions into 'kernel' sentences in order to facilitate translation (cf. for example Nida, 1964; Nida & Taber, 1969). However, Chomsky's theoretical model of grammar was not the only one to gain currency. In the UK, Michael Halliday put forward his proposal for a Scale and Category Grammar, which in turn provided the impetus for Catford to develop an alternative approach to translation as outlined in *A Linguistic Theory of Translation* (1965). Just as Chomsky provided us with a blueprint for a linguistic theory to be used for the description of natural language, so Nida and Catford attempted to present us with linguistic theories to account for the process of translation. And although practising translators may not have found them of immediate use, taking issue with some of the proposals, they remain, nevertheless, systematic attempts to capture and formulate in linguistic terms the differences between source language (SL) and target language (TL) and the problems which are likely to confront the translator in moving from one language to the other.

It is interesting to note that the move towards applying linguistic theory to translation had been foreshadowed in the 1950s in foreign language teaching and learning by Robert Lado's attempt to put language teaching, language testing and language-learning experiments on a scientific basis (Lado, 1957). The 'science' of his approach was a structuralist comparison of the learner's L1 and the target L2, generally known as the contrastive analysis hypothesis (CAH), which could, it was initially claimed, lead to a rationalisation of teaching through a prediction of areas of difficulty and learner error. By the 1970s, however, the CAH had ceded its position to more developmentally-based approaches to L2 acquisition, since the predictions made proved to be unreliable.

These early attempts to formulate a theory of language teaching and translation were ambitious in nature, which is perhaps why they were not entirely successful. But linguistics may be useful to the language teacher as well as to the translator in a different way, as a source of explanation for specific problems. In applied linguistics, this took the form of attempting to explain learners' errors rather than predict them (Wardhaugh, 1974). And in the case of translation, there are in fact many subdivisions of linguistics which could be of immediate interest to the translator. One obvious area is sociolinguistics, a branch of linguistics which provides us with information about the relation of language to social situation. When, for instance, the translator faces the task of having to translate a source text (ST) written in dialect, it might be helpful to gain a closer awareness of the relationship between dialect and social structure in the TL culture. It may be the case that certain dialects are more closely linked to social class than others, as perhaps most famously immortalised by Bernard Shaw in *Pygmalion*. In some cases the availability of a particular dialect in the TL may even provide new-found opportunities for representing sociolects in the ST, normally difficult to capture in translation. This appears, for instance, to be the case when the works of American writers such as Tennessee Williams and Edward Albee are translated into Québécois, where a proletarisation of language in the target text (TT) makes possible a close match with the original, not easily obtainable in translation into standard French (Brisset, 1989).

Problems related to dialects are, however, not the only difficulties facing the translator at the level of the text. It is frequently necessary to consider questions relating to text linguistics, including the analysis of thematic structure, coherence and cohesion, and pragmatics (cf. Hatim & Mason, 1990; Bell, 1991; Baker, 1992). Recent interest in pragmatics, in particular cross-cultural pragmatics, has also pointed to the relevance of speech acts such as apologies, requests, compliments etc., all expressed in accordance with different formulae, depending on the language used. Speech acts, including awareness of these formulae and their use in different languages thus constitute another area of clear interest to translators, in particular to the translator of dialogue (cf. Anderman, 1993). Yet further attempts to find a coherent model for translation drawing on findings in linguistics have looked to Sperber and Wilson's relevance theory, as for instance Gutt (1991).

Translation Studies: A Multidiscipline

In so far as it provides a framework for a systematic description of language, linguistics seems to be a discipline of obvious interest to the field of translation studies. However, as interest in translation studies started to grow, so did the awareness of the importance of other disciplines. Around 1980, a new approach was making itself known which was both interdisciplinary as well as culturally oriented (cf. Leppihalme, 1994: 1). Bassnett-McGuire (1991) and Snell-Hornby (1988), for instance, pointed to the interdisciplinary nature of translation studies with the emphasis on texts in their 'macro-context' (Snell-Hornby, 1991: 15). An increasing number of literary scholars also started to turn their attention to translations as instruments of mediation and influence between national literatures. The observation that translators from different cultures and different time periods would render a work in translation differently showed that a framework for historical-relative and sociocultural models of translation was emerging (Heylen, 1993).

Nida too abandoned his earlier commitment to a 'science of translating' (1964) and voiced his support for an interdisciplinary approach to translation studies, drawing on findings from a number of different disciplines (Nida, 1985). By the mid 1980s Nida appears far less concerned with 'translation theory', 'the science of translating' or 'translatology' than he did 20 years earlier. Instead he stresses the importance of the use of language for communicative purposes and the processes involved in interlingual communication. The term 'science' loses the rigour with which it was previously applied and is used quite differently, simply as anything which can be subjected to careful, analytical and exhaustive study. In fact, Nida now seems to prefer to talk about the process of translation — or interlingual communication — as a kind of 'technology' in which we draw upon a number of disciplines in combination. In this way, according to Nida, the translator closely resembles the engineer in the process of building a bridge, who must draw upon knowledge gained from other fields such as physics, metallurgy and mathematics in order to erect his construction. Similarly, in order to arrive at the translation, the finished product, the translator also seeks support from a number of disciplines.

There is little doubt that the translator or Nida's bridge-building engineer will need help from other subject specialists in order to arrive at the finished product. Legal translation may, for instance, call for the knowledge of a legally-trained expert; economic texts, to take another example, are not likely to be translated successfully without some insight into economics. This subject expertise, however, is primarily focused on concepts and their relations, embodied in words and realised in the transference of terms from one language to another. While the debate relating to the word-for-word versus sense-for-sense principles of translation — more recently extended to include text-for-text — may have raged since Antiquity, the fact still remains that words occupy a position of unique importance as the basic building material of the text, the content words forming the 'bricks' and the function words the 'mortar' (Aitchison, 1994: 106–9), ready for use by the bridge-builder/translator.

Refocusing on Words

While in translating a text we may refer problems in transferring words from the ST to the TT to the higher level of the text, we cannot begin to translate a text without reference to the word. Indeed, the authority for many translation problems of both decoding and encoding is often the surrounding words in either the ST or the new TT which is under creation, since the way words interact with their neighbours — so-called syntagmatic relations — as well as paradigmatic relations, that is the interaction with their sub- or superordinates or equivalents, plays an essential role in the cohesive construction of a text. Translation has in fact been described as 'something people do with words' (Chesterman, 1985: 5), and J.L. Austin's seminal work on speech acts was called *How to do Things with Words* (1962). Reflecting on a more prosaic level, the normal custom for charging for translating services is by word count, a fact keenly illustrating the fact that the translator's livelihood is, literally, dependent on the 'word'.

The years immediately following the Chomskyan revolution, however, saw limited interest in the lexicon among linguists while the study of grammar and syntax rapidly gained in popularity, in particular the application of a theoretical framework to various syntactic domains in a number of different languages. Since one of Chomsky's main contributions to linguistics had been to emphasise the commonalities of natural languages rather than their differences, great interest was generated by the prospect of pinpointing linguistic features which were shared by a wide range of languages. With the ultimate aim of establishing a set of language universals, different syntactic structures were investigated, such as negation, the imperative, and active/passive constructions, in English as well as in other languages, and the system of rules relating to their formation documented.

At about the same time interest turned to the field of first language acquisition, where the same areas of grammar were similarly subjected to analysis. This time, linguists focused their attention on the rules pertaining to the different stages in the learning process of young children acquiring their first language (L1). This in turn was followed by a growing interest in second language (L2) acquisition and in the study of children as well as adults learning other languages in addition to their own (L2, L3, etc.).

While initial interest in language acquisition was primarily concerned with grammar and syntax, the last few decades have seen a gradual shift towards the study of different aspects of vocabulary. An increasing number of linguists have started to turn their attention to the study of the lexicon, and the plethora of findings now emerging suggests that this field of enquiry is beginning to acquire a prominent position within the field of linguistics. As a result, interest has started to focus on how we learn and use words in L1 as well as in L2 acquisition.

In the field of translation studies, however, where the impact from disciplines other than linguistics has been felt for some time, only ripples, if anything, have so far been felt from the findings of recent work on the L1 or the L2 lexicon. While recent theoretical work in linguistics has unearthed a wealth of information about the way we use and acquire words in our own and other languages, this has, in the main, not been considered in relation to translation.

The papers contained in the present volume all deal with some aspect of vocabulary. On the one hand, observations on words in the mental lexicon, particularly in connection with L1 and L2 acquisition, are presented and then explored in relation to translation. On the other hand, the translation of words and their representation in dictionaries leads to consideration of implications for the language learner. The intention has been to show that these new areas, so far untapped for complementary research findings, might not only draw on, but also enrich a multidisciplinary field such as translation studies.

Overview

Jean Aitchison's chapter, 'Taming the Wilderness: Words in the Mental Lexicon', serves as an introduction, highlighting five topics as being of special interest: vocabulary size, word storage, links between words, the acquisition process, and word retrieval. With respect to the first topic, Aitchison provides us with some information about vocabulary size which shows that the mental lexicon is in fact much larger than has been assumed. While for instance the much-praised 'talking chimps' each possess around 200 vocabulary items, a typical five-year-old knows about 25 times as many words. This in turn points to the conclusions that many people's assumptions about vocabulary size should be revised, and that expectations about the number of words that must be readily available in a translator's repertoire need to be raised.

The second issue singled out for attention is the way in which all these words are stored and remembered, a not insignificant problem given that an educated speaker of English uses an estimated 50,000 lexical items. Aitchison propounds the now favoured view that rather than having fixed, precise meanings, words have 'fuzzy edges' (Lakoff, 1972: 183) and that humans work from prototypes when learning the meaning of new words. Statistically, there is considerable agreement on the degree to which an item is considered prototypical within a particular culture. However, the ability to rank items in an adult manner takes time to acquire, and the intermediate stages in acquiring this ranking have, in turn, implications for language learning and for translation, which requires cross-cultural comparisons of prototype hierarchies. Children often differ from adults with respect to categorisation, a fact not always considered by the writers of school textbooks, who sometimes choose non-prototypical members of a category in an effort to make the material interesting. And for a translator, it may sometimes be more important to replace a prototypical instance with another prototypical instance, rather than with the exact lexical equivalent.

Aitchison also makes brief mention of an offshoot of prototype theory concerned with covert mental models, which may not exist in the real world. One such case is the word *week*, which is envisaged by British speakers as consisting of five working days and two rest days, even if their own lives do not conform to this prototype. The proposal that these covert models may be revealed through our everyday use of metaphors is later picked up by Anderman in her discussion of the notion of prototype in relation to translation.

Prototypes and covert mental models are, however, not the only issues of interest with respect to the mechanisms involved in word storage. Words also have relationships with other words. According to Aitchison, two types of link seem to have priority in the mental lexicon: collocational links and ties between coordinates. Collocation refers to the habitual association of one word with another, as in *silly ass*, where the combination of the adjective *silly* with the noun *ass* tells us that what is referred to is not a four-legged animal but rather, in this particular instance, a two-legged human.

Coordinates, on the other hand, are names of items within the same set, belonging to the same word class, such as *chair*, *table* and *sofa*. Overall, Aitchison suggests, an investigation into the links between words indicates that native speakers remember lexical items in context. These observations are then reinforced by her discussion of how children acquire words in the first place, dealing in particular with over- and undergeneralisations. In the former case, children extend the meaning of a word too widely, as in the case of small children referring to all four-legged animals as *bow-wow*, whereas in the latter case they restrict the meaning to too small a range of words. This happens, for example, when a child believes that the word *kitten* refers only to the family cat and not to all recently-born cats. Underextension also appears to characterise adult learning, where full mastery normally follows on from previous usage within a limited context.

However, when the learning process is over and the words are stored, they have to be retrieved from the mental lexicon whenever we need to use them. How then do we go about finding the right word? According to Aitchison, who concludes her chapter with a discussion of this issue, there is evidence to suggest that when we start our search for the right word, we unknowingly activate many more words than we actually need. It may be the case that lexical items from all the languages we may know are potentially interconnected, and that we only manage to find a particular word in one language by suppressing unwanted words for that particular item in other languages familiar to us.

Although as yet tentative, these recent findings relating to the mental lexicon seem to have interesting implications for anyone concerned with vocabulary, and the chapters that follow all bring up related themes and ideas for discussion in the context of language learning, teaching and translation.

Paul Meara's chapter provides a summary of the major empirical research into L2 vocabulary acquisition carried out between 1900 and 1960, as well as a critical analysis of some of the issues to which these studies point. Such papers are now enjoying a resurgence in popularity as authoritative references and, although Meara ostensibly discusses work on vocabulary acquisition carried out some 30 or 40 years ago, many of the comments made apply equally well to work that has appeared more recently. There is, as he points out, 'little sign that any of the work carried out since 1960 has had any serious impact on course design or teaching practice'.

The first problem discussed by Meara concerns the individual differences that may exist in relation to L2 vocabulary skills. We know that such differences in L1 vocabulary skills are very large, and there is reason to believe that the same sort of variation might apply in the case of L2 learners. What we do not know, however, is the extent of this variation.

The second problem results from the restricted range of languages involved in the studies discussed and the fact that broad generalisations have been made on the basis of this narrow selection. In particular, the concentration on English is bound to distort the picture, as English vocabulary 'seems to be inordinately large compared to the basic vocabularies of other languages'. Here Meara anticipates Newmark's discussion of the difficulties of translation out of English, owing to its multifaceted vocabulary.

The third problem with which Meara is concerned relates to the lack of attention that has been given to the lexicon. No attempts appear to have been made in these major studies to assess how the overall structure of the L2 lexicon develops, or how, say, a small lexicon might differ from a large one. Far from approaching it as the complex, interlocking structure that Aitchison's chapter gives us reason to believe it is, the lexicon is simply viewed as nothing but an unstructured list of words, recalling, we might add, the bilingual lists of vocabulary so often favoured in the language learning classroom and in some translators' glossaries.

While Aitchison is concerned with the mechanisms involved when we try to find a word, Meara draws attention to the limited discussion that seems to exist with respect to what it means to 'know a word'. Most current research still looks at vocabulary as discrete items which can be marked as correct or incorrect on the basis of simple recognition or production tests.

Teachers of translation concerned with course design may, however, be interested to learn about the findings related to subjects' learning and forgetting of words as presented in vocabulary lists. Results clearly seem to indicate that cognate L2 words are learnt much better than non- or semi-cognate words. This, it would seem, should provide some food for thought for designers of course curricula for trainee translators. It is now common practice for trainees on postgraduate courses in translation to be introduced to additional languages *ab initio*. The fact that cognate constructions, as well as words, are learnt with greater ease as well as speed would seem to indicate that in order to reach a high level of linguistic competence in a minimum period of time, would-be translators are likely to derive optimal benefit if *ab initio* language courses place a premium on offering languages closely related to those with which students are already familiar.

Gunilla Anderman's chapter, 'The Word is My Oyster — the Language Learner and the Translator', resumes the discussion where Aitchison left off with respect to the proposal that humans work from prototypes when learning the meaning of new words. She starts by briefly discussing the notion of prototype as well as work on categorisation, which has shown that certain members of a given category seem to be generally perceived as more 'typical' than others, although adults and children differ in their analyses. Indeed, children go through a number of stages of development in their gradual approximation to the adult system. Just as children need to revise their notions about prototypes, so also do translators moving between languages. Anderman illustrates this by reference to the word *kick* in English, which expresses two concepts at once, namely, motion and manner. Not only is this difficult for a child to grasp, it also poses problems for the translator going into Romance languages, where manner normally needs to be expressed through an additional constituent. In this way, *They drove into the courtyard* would need reorganisation into *They entered the courtyard by car* for translation into French — often a stumbling block for L2 learners, as any teacher of French knows only too well.

Picking up on the close link between second language learning and translation, the chapter proceeds to consider the application of prototype theory to L2 acquisition and its implications for translation. Of particular interest here are the observations that have been made in relation to a form of prototype effect commonly known in linguistics as 'markedness'. Here the concept of markedness is used to show that in a given category, such as, for instance, the word class consisting of verbs, some core or 'nuclear' verbs are used much more frequently than others. If, for instance, we turn to a specific group of verbs such as the verbs of motion, we find that *go* constitutes such a nuclear verb. Nuclear verbs seem to be favoured at an early age by both L1 and L2 learners, and are likely to occur with great frequency in everyday, colloquial language. Yet studies of original and translated texts show distortions of word frequency patterns in the TT which may result in the stylistic awkwardness not infrequently associated with texts in translation. Greater familiarity on the part of the translator with the way language is acquired and used would, in all likelihood, help to counteract this type of manifestation of so-called 'translationese'. As we have seen, one source of information shedding light on this subject is the field of language acquisition.

The chapter then goes on to examine attempts that have already been made to apply the concept of prototype to translation. Such proposals include applying a form of prototype analysis to representative samples of texts in the TL in order to arrive at a textual profile containing typical syntactic and lexical features which may serve as a guide in the creation of the TT, and matching equivalents according to five basic groups of prototypes, where the task becomes increasingly more difficult as lexical items become more culture bound.

In concluding her chapter, Anderman refers to Aitchison's discussion of covert mental models and the suggestion that these may be revealed through the use of everyday metaphors. As this in turn may help us move closer to an understanding of metaphors, whether they are universal or specific to a certain language and culture, there would seem little doubt that this offshoot of prototype theory might also yield further information of interest to the translator.

Peter Newmark's chapter, 'Looking at English Words in Translation', considers the theme of equivalence and the extent to which it is possible to establish perfect translation equivalence between lexical items in the SL and the TL. English is viewed as occupying a special place as regards translation equivalence, having a much larger vocabulary than many other languages, as discussed by Meara with respect to L2 acquisition. Through numerous examples from European languages, Newmark argues that, thanks to its 'triple principal antecedents', the English language is particularly rich in alternative available forms of items in most word classes, and also allows for greater flexibility in the expression of register. It is this richness, Newmark argues, that might make it difficult to find appropriate equivalents translating out of English. He views this as being linked to the adoption of loan-words into English, resulting in an increased capacity for the language to adapt and evolve. However, this ongoing enrichment is not considered to be limited to lexis, and Newmark proceeds to demonstrate flexibility in the verbal system through an illustration of the different uses to which the *-ing* form of English verbs may be put. Further examples develop this concept of the richness of English grammar in permitting the creation of new words, with detailed discussion of such examples. The question of words in translation is addressed and illustrated throughout with a contrastive approach, concluding that while translation out of English may present a number of problems, English has greater resources for representing the meaning of other languages.

The difficulty which Newmark observes of translating out of English, with its greater lexical and, in some cases, grammatical flexibility, may also be related to the problems faced by L2 learners in their use of English. Confronted with apparent synonyms such as *go down* and *descend*, Romance learners, for example, tend to choose the usually inappropriate but cognate Latin derivative, as in *He descended the stairs*. On the grammatical front, problems with the verbal system are well known to teachers of English as L2. And so, what makes English 'often less amenable to translation than other languages', as Newmark argues, also makes it more difficult in some respects for L2 learners to acquire and use appropriately.

A notable by-product of the increasing attention given to the expanding vocabulary of English is the number of English dictionaries that have appeared over the last 20 years specifically devoted to neologisms. In the chapter, 'Lexical Innovation: Neologism and Dictionaries', John Ayto examines what light dictionaries may cast on the processes of lexical innovation. He begins by distinguishing between two sorts of new-word dictionaries, compiled with very different aims in mind and using different methods. First there is the supplement to an existing dictionary, typically a large academic one which sets out to contribute to a complete historical record, such as the supplement to the *Oxford English Dictionary* (1972–1985). Then there is the independent self-contained dictionary recording neologisms from a particular delimited period, such as Ayto's own *Longman Register of New Words*, Volumes 1 and 2 (1989, 1990). This dichotomy, then, determines two very different approaches to the monitoring of new vocabulary. While the supplementary variety aims to be exhaustive, the self-contained dictionary of neologisms tends to be more selective.

What then can we learn from dictionaries about the process of word formation in English? It seems that over half of all the 'new' lexical items appear to be formed by reshuffling existing elements through processes known as derivation and compounding. And if we then add semantic change, that is, the development of new meanings in established words, 75% of the total is accounted for. Surprisingly, acronyms and coinages, however popular they may seem to be, make up only an insignificant percentage of the total.

Another question on which dictionaries may throw some light is the durability of new coinages. In answer to how many neologisms survive, Ayto suggests a survival rate equivalent to roughly 2% of the entries in a large desk dictionary, or approximately 3.3% of the average educated person's mental lexicon.

Neologisms naturally reflect current concerns and trends in society. In particular they reveal which areas of activity are most fertile in the creation of new vocabulary. In the 1970s computing was well to the fore, while in the 1980s it was overtaken by the financial world. Terminology relating to the City of London outnumbered all other areas. Not surprisingly, the big crash in October 1987 was followed by a dramatic drop in the incidence of financial neologisms.

Dedicated dictionaries of neologisms provide an invaluable service to language learners as well as to translators. Not only do they help to bridge the gap between the appearance of new words and their inclusion in standard dictionaries, they also record ephemeral items that might not even make it into standard dictionaries.

While a number of chapters in the present volume show that the translator stands to gain from findings in the fields of L1 as well as L2 acquisition, the concluding contribution from Margaret Rogers sets out to show that the converse may also be possible. In 'Beyond the Dictionary: the Translator, the L2 Learner and the Computer', she suggests that some of the recent developments in technology, currently breaking new ground for translators, may also be of interest to language learners. As she points out, solutions to pedagogical problems have often been sought optimistically in technology. While the 1960s and the 1970s were the decades of the language laboratory, the 1980s saw the wide-scale introduction of the computer into language teaching. Now the idea of a 'workbench' as a set of integrated computer tools to be used according to need is becoming familiar in the fields of translation, terminology, lexicography and language for special purposes. Based on this model, Rogers' proposal entails a workbench-for-words, which allows for a user-driven approach to L2 vocabulary learning and use through databases, dictionaries and texts accessible in the electronic medium.

Rogers further elaborates on Aitchison's discussion about the way words are stored and organised in the mental lexicon. Referring to Meara (1984), Rogers points out that the possibilities considered in relation to the 'ordering' of items in the L2 mental lexicon are similar to those discussed for L1, and include some sort of thesaurus-based system. Having considered some issues of pedagogy in the teaching of meaning in L2 vocabulary, pointing to ways in which the linguistic analysis of meaning as associative networks has been pedagogically applied, she turns her attention to different reference works which attempt to codify lexical meanings. She concludes that while semantically-based dictionaries, where meaning serves as an organising principle in some way, may go some way towards meeting learners' needs, we must look further afield in order to provide greater opportunities for learners themselves to explore lexical patterns and to make their own lexica. The proposed solution is to follow the current trend in the use of the computer to assist translators rather than to replace them: in other words, the trend to favour computer-assisted human translation rather than full machine translation. In the field of L2 vocabulary learning and teaching, Rogers concludes, this leads us to seek a solution in the user-driven workbench notion rather than in full intelligent computer-assisted language learning.

Conclusion

In this chapter we have been concerned to describe how, as a relatively new discipline drawing on related subjects, translation studies enjoyed from very early on a close association with linguistics, in which ambitious attempts were made to systematically link the two. At the time the focus was on syntax, the lexicon being given limited attention. More recently, however, interest has shifted, the study of vocabulary having attracted increasing attention. We have attempted to show that the study of words may be approached from a number of perspectives, linked to translation on the one hand and language learning on the other, and that the findings in these areas may benefit both disciplines. But although until now it is translation studies which have gained from the findings of linguistics, perhaps in the future linguistics and studies of language learning will make greater reference to translation, one of the most interesting cognitive activities undertaken in the realm of language.

References

AITCHISON, J. 1994, *Words in the Mind: An Introduction to the Mental Lexicon* 2nd edn. Oxford: Blackwell.
ANDERMAN, G. 1993, Translation and speech acts. In Y. GAMBIER and J. TOMMOLA (eds) *Translation and Knowledge*. Scandinavian Symposium on Translation Theory IV, Turku, 4–6 June 1992 (pp. 377–87). Turku: Turku University.
AUSTIN, J.L. 1962, *How to do Things with Words*. Oxford: Clarendon Press.
AYTO, J. 1989, *Longman Register of New Words* Vol. 1. London: Longman.
— 1990, *Longman Register of New Words* Vol. 2. London: Longman.
BAKER, M. 1992, *In Other Words. A Coursebook on Translation*. London: Routledge.
BASSNETT-MCGUIRE, S. 1980/1991, *Translation Studies*. London: Routledge.
BELL, R. 1991, *Translation and Translating. Theory and Practice*. London: Routledge.
BRISSET, A. 1989, In search of a target language: The politics of theatre translation in Quebec. *Target* 1, 9–27.
CATFORD, J.C. 1965, *A Linguistic Theory of Translation. An Essay in Applied Linguistics*. London: Oxford University Press.

CHESTERMAN, A. (ed) 1985, *Readings in Translation Theory*. Helsinki: Oy Finn Lectura Ab.
GUTT, E-A. 1991, *Translation and Relevance. Cognition and Context*. Oxford: Blackwell.
HATIM, B. and MASON, I. 1990, *Discourse and the Translator*. London: Longman.
HEYLEN, R. 1993, *Translation, Poetics and the Stage. Six French Hamlets*. London: Routledge.
LADO, R. 1957, *Linguistics Across Cultures*. Ann Arbor, MI.: University of Michigan Press.
LAKOFF, G. 1972, Hedges: A study in meaning criteria and the logic of fuzzy concepts. *Papers of the Eighth Chicago Linguistics Society* (pp.183–228).
LEPPIHALME, R. 1994, *Culture Bumps. On the Translation of Allusions*. English Department Studies. Helsinki: University of Helsinki.
MEARA, P. 1984, The study of lexis in interlanguage. In A. DAVIES, C. CRIPER and A.P.R. HOWATT (eds) *Interlanguage* (pp.225–35). Edinburgh: Edinburgh University Press.
NIDA, E.A. 1964, *Toward a Science of Translating. With Special Reference to Principles and Procedures Involved in Bible Translating*. Leiden: E.J. Brill.
—— 1985, Transcript of an interview with S. Chau, November 9, 1985 *Hong Kong Translation Forum 6*.
NIDA, E.A. and TABER, C.R. 1969, *The Theory and Practice of Translation. Help for Translators* Vol 8. Prepared under the auspices of the United Bible Societies. Leiden: E. J. Brill.
SNELL-HORNBY, M. 1988, *Translation Studies: An Integrated Approach*. Amsterdam: John Benjamins.
—— 1991, Translation Studies — Art, Science or Utopia? In K. VAN LEUWEN-ZWART and T. NAAIJKEENS (eds) *Translation Studies: The State of the Art*. Proceedings of the First James S. Holmes Symposium on Translation Studies (pp. 5–12) Amsterdam: Rodopi.
WARDHAUGH, R. 1974, The contrastive analysis hypothesis. In J. SCHUMANN and N. STENSON (eds) *New Frontiers in Second Language Learning* (pp. 111–19). Rowley, MA: Newbury House.

2 Taming the Wilderness: Words in the Mental Lexicon

JEAN AITCHISON

> I have put my faith in language — hence the panic when a simple word eludes me... I control the world so long as I can name it. Which is why children must chase language before they do anything else, tame the wilderness by describing it.

This quotation from Penelope Lively's novel *Moon Tiger* (Lively, 1987/1988: 51) describes a common feeling, that the ability to cope with the world is dependent on having words available for describing it. But in spite of a widespread belief that vocabulary is important, there is considerable ignorance about how the mind deals with words. This is perhaps because those professionally concerned with linguistics have for the last few decades laid greater stress on syntax. Words have been treated as a somewhat uninteresting jumble of miscellanea which speakers learn 'item by item, in a more or less rote fashion' (Katz & Fodor, 1963: 183).

Recently, this viewpoint has shown signs of changing. There has been a wave of new psycholinguistic work on the 'mental lexicon' — the dictionary which we presumably all carry in our minds. This chapter (which is based on Aitchison 1994) draws attention to findings that seem particularly relevant to those actively working with translation and/or the learning of vocabulary. It uses English as the language of exemplification, although the matters discussed have a wider application. In the following pages, five topics have been highlighted as being of special interest: vocabulary size, word storage, links between words, the acquisition process and word retrieval.

How Many Words?

Dean Farrar, a nineteenth-century intellectual, once eavesdropped on some peasants picking apples, and conjectured that they used only 100 words between them. They managed on this low number, he surmised, because 'the same coarse expletives recurred with a horrible frequency in the place of every single part of speech' (Farrar, 1865: 59). This anecdote illustrates a tendency that is still widespread: the underestimation of vocabulary size. For example, a newspaper columnist confused the 'defining vocabulary' used by the *Longman Dictionary of Contemporary English* (about 3,000 words) with the number used by an average English speaker. Another popular misconception is that the size of a person's lexicon is around two-thirds of Shakespeare's vocabulary, whose plays contain about 30,000 different words. And a 'guestimate' of 20,000 words for an average person's vocabulary is found in several oldish psychology textbooks, although sources for this figure are obscure.

But these numbers are far too low. According to recent research, the average university student knows, and can potentially use, more than 50,000 words (Miller & Gildea, 1987: 86). A word is assumed to be a headword in a good dictionary, and so includes all inflectional forms, and derivatives whose form and meanings are fully deducible from the base (e.g. *talk, talked, talker* are all subsumed under the headword *talk*).

Moving backwards, an average 13-year-old possibly knows around 20,000 words (Aitchison & Koppel, 1990), and an average five-year-old around 5,000, a figure averaged from several diary studies. This figure implies that children acquire on average 10 words a day between the ages of 5 and 20 — although Miller and Gildea (1987) put the figure even higher. In reality, vocabulary acquisition is unlikely to spread evenly over the intervening years. For example, there appears to be a leap at around age 12–13 (Aitchison & Koppel, 1990).

To put these figures into perspective, a typical five-year-old probably knows 25 times as many words as any one of the much-praised 'talking chimps', who each possess around 200 vocabulary items. A typical student can use the equivalent of two-thirds of the *Concise Oxford Dictionary*, which claims to contain around 75,000 entries.

The moral of this is that many people's assumptions about vocabulary size should be revised, and expectations need to be raised about the number of English words that must be readily available in a translator's repertoire.

But how, exactly, are so many words stored and remembered? This is the topic of the next section.

Good Birds and Better Birds

'Words have basic inalienable meanings, departure from which is either conscious metaphor or inexcusable vulgarity', according to the novelist Evelyn Waugh (quoted in Green, 1982: 254). The view that words have fixed, precise meanings goes back at least to Aristotle, and is enshrined in the traditional attempt to define word meaning in terms of 'necessary and sufficient conditions'. It is sometimes spoken of as the 'checklist' view, since speakers of a language are envisaged as metaphorically checking off a number of fixed conditions.

Most psycholinguists now regard this view as outmoded. It works only occasionally, mainly for technical terms such as *triangle*, or in cases where a definition might be consciously specified for a particular purpose, as in the following bureaucratic definition of a cow: 'A cow is a female bovine animal which has borne a calf, or has, in the opinion of the Minister, been brought into a herd to replace one which has borne a calf' (quoted in a letter to *The Times*).

But in most cases, 'natural language concepts have vague boundaries and fuzzy edges' (Lakoff, 1972: 183). This has been known for quite a long time. More than fifteen years ago, the sociolinguist William Labov showed that in naming various containers, people not only disagreed with one another over bowls, cups and vases, but were inconsistent from day to day (Labov, 1973). Certain shapes were clear instances of particular containers, he found, but others varied, especially with their use: something might be a bowl when it contained potatoes, but a vase when it held flowers. And over thirty years ago, the philosopher Wittgenstein pointed out the 'family resemblance' syndrome, using the word *game* as an example (Wittgenstein, 1958). Every game has similarities with some other game — ring-a-roses and tennis involve physical activity; tennis and chess require a winner; chess and patience are normally played indoors — but there is no one factor which links them all.

Prototype theory, developed in the mid 1970s, deals with both the 'fuzzy edges' phenomenon and the 'family resemblance' syndrome. Human beings, it transpires, probably work from prototypical instances (Rosch, 1975). A robin, for example, is regarded as a prototypical bird by many American speakers of English, and a blackbird by many British speakers. People analyse the characteristics of this prototype, and allow anything that sufficiently resembles the prototype to belong to the same category. This accounts for how humans deal with oddities and damaged examples. It shows why humans can accept penguins and emus as birds, and why three-legged unstriped vegetarian tigers can still be tigers (cf. for a summary, Taylor, 1989; Aitchison, 1994).

Prototypes, however, are not a panacea, and there is considerable controversy about their nature (Geeraerts, 1989; Aitchison, 1994). But whatever the shadowy constitution of a prototype, there seems little doubt that humans do not rank all members of a category equally (Rosch, 1975). They judge some to be 'better' than others: a robin or blackbird is a better bird than a duck, which in turn is better than a penguin. And statistically, there is considerable agreement on the various rankings within a particular culture.

However, an ability to rank items in an adult manner takes time, and the intermediate stages in acquiring this ranking have implications for language learning and translation. When asked to select the 'best examples' of a category, English 11–14-year-olds differed from adults in a number of ways. The youngest children did not make any consistent selection, and older ones tended to give a top ranking to items which were important to them. English children tended to give high priority to potatoes on the vegetable list (they liked them) and to parrots on the bird list (they found them more eye-catching) — although some of the unpredictable responses turned out to be due to pictures in books. Textbooks, in an effort to be interesting, had sometimes selected non-prototypical members as representatives of a category, such as a peacock or parrot as an example of a bird. Therefore teachers and translators need to be aware that in keeping readers' interest, they may also be preventing them from acquiring the cultural prototype. Furthermore, since prototypes vary across cultures, it may sometimes be more important when translating to replace a prototypical instance with another prototypical instance, rather than with the exact lexical equivalent.

It follows that the ranking of items within a category differs from culture to culture. For instance, English speakers expect vehicles to have wheels, and regard cars and buses as prototypical. French speakers are less fussy about the wheels, and many accept even skis and lifts as good instances of 'un véhicule'.

The French view of vehicles also shows that category boundaries vary across cultures, since skis would probably be outside the category 'vehicle' for many English speakers. In order to probe covert differences in category boundaries, English children were compared with fluent non-native speakers of English (Aitchison, 1992a). 11–14-year-olds were asked questions such as: 'Is a walnut a fruit?' 'Is a lettuce a vegetable?' 'Is a goose a bird?' Their responses gradually approximated to the adult norm, with answers indistinguishable from those of adults by the age of 13 (in the cases above, no, no and yes, respectively). But even advanced foreign learners of English were influenced by their native language, even though they were unaware of this. Italians, for example, tended to claim that a walnut was a fruit (a dried fruit), and that a goose was not a bird, on the grounds that it was a fowl.

More recently, as an offshoot of prototype theory, attention has shifted to mental models which may not exist in the real world. The word *week*, for example, is envisaged by British English speakers as consisting of seven days, of which five days are working days and two are rest days. This prototypical week exists in their minds even if their own lives do not conform to it. An Inca, on the other hand, had a mental model of a nine-day week, of which eight days were working days. The ninth day was market day, on which the king changed wives.

Mental models can therefore differ considerably across cultures. The problem arises as to how these covert models can be identified. One possibility is that they can be revealed via metaphors. English speakers possibly view anger as heated liquid in a container (Lakoff, 1987): *Paul seethed with rage; Mary's anger boiled over; Henry exploded.* Some metaphors and models have a physiological basis, and so may be universal, but particular cultures tend to stress some physiological symptoms at the expense of others (Aitchison, 1992b). This has become a promising field of enquiry (e.g. Wierzbicka, 1992).

But word storage is not just a case of acquiring a heap of prototypes and discovering the ranking of other items within the same category. Nor is it just a case of building abstract mental models. In addition, words have relationships with other words in the vocabulary.

Why Can't Eggs be Rancid?

Yellow is a colour. It has links with other colours, and with the word *colour*. It occurs in phrases such as *yellow fever*, and also has some rough synonyms, such as *golden, amber, flaxen*. These multifarious connections are unlikely to be equally important (cf. on links in general, Cruse, 1986; Miller, 1990; Lehrer & Kittay, 1992; Levin & Pinker, 1992; Aitchison, 1994).

Traditional vocabulary books tend to stress the relationship between hyponyms and superordinates, as when *red, yellow*, and *blue* are presented under the label *colour*. But, somewhat counterintuitively, superordinates are not particularly important in the mental lexicon, except in a few clearcut cases. Often, coordinates (co-hyponyms) are used to refer to a category, rather than a superordinate: people talk about 'brothers and sisters' rather than their *siblings; rain and snow* rather than *precipitation; knives and forks* rather than *cutlery.*

Two types of link seem to have priority in the mental lexicon: collocational links, on the one hand, and ties between co-ordinates (co-hyponyms) on the other. Collocation is the habitual association of a word with other words that occur alongside it. These associations are so strong that a popular television game exploits them, assuming that a word such as *star* will elicit a standard set of responses, such as *starlight, stardust, star wars*. Furthermore, English speakers are highly sensitive to which one of several near-synonyms collocates with a particular word. *Rancid, rank* and *rotten* tend to have somewhat similar definitions in dictionaries, but each is attached to its own set of lexical items. So English speakers refer to *rancid butter, rotten eggs,* and *rank weeds*. And verbs, as is well known, determine the subsequent structure: you have to *put* something somewhere, as the car in the garage, or the plate on the table; you cannot just **put the car,* or **put the plate* (cf. Levin & Pinker, 1992).

Ties between coordinates (co-hyponyms) are particularly strong for adults. These are items that belong to the same word class and are on the same level of detail within a semantic area, as with *cup, plate, saucer,* or *tulip, daffodil, crocus*. These links are shown by 'selection errors', cases in which people accidentally select the wrong word, as in *brother* for *sister, aunt* for *niece, tomorrow* for *yesterday*. Further evidence comes from research with brain-damaged patients. Stroke victims may call a lemon an *apple* or *orange*. They have not necessarily forgotten the word name, but the various names within a set may have become confused, so that these patients may have genuinely forgotten which word applies to which piece of fruit, just as some normal speakers cannot remember which is which among various breeds of dog or makes of car (Butterworth, Howard & McLoughlin, 1984).

Some (controversial) work with aphasics suggests that different topic areas can be detached from one another. For example, one now-famous stroke victim found that he could name just about everything except fruit and vegetables (Hart, Berndt & Caramazza, 1985). Another could name items of clothing, but not types of cloth. A third failed to comprehend the words *carrot* and *needle,* but could cope with *pact* and *knowledge* (Warrington, 1981).

Overall, therefore, an investigation into the links between words suggests that native speakers remember lexical items in context, within topic areas. Words are not as interchangeable as was once assumed. These observations can be reinforced by a consideration of how children acquire words in the first place.

Starting out

The nineteenth century psychologist James Sully drew attention to a 'curious and often quaintly pretty' feature of 'the early tussle with language'. This was the extension of names by children in 'new and surprising directions', such as the use of the word *pin* to mean a crumb, a fly and a caterpillar (Sully, 1897, in Bar-Adon & Leopold, 1971: 37). Such observations are widespread.

However, in recent years two findings have emerged. First, overgeneralisation (extending a word too widely) occurs less frequently than undergeneralisation (restricting a word to too small a range). Secondly, overgeneralisation is not the simple matter it is sometimes assumed to be (cf. Clark, 1993; Aitchison, 1994 for an overview).

Underextensions are rarely remarked upon since they result in accurate usage, but scattered anecdotes and careful probing suggest that they are very common. For example, 20-month-old Hildegarde refused to accept that *white* applied to the pages of a book, since she associated it only with 'snow' (Leopold, 1948, in Bar-Adon & Leopold, 1971: 98). Another child associated the word *deep* with swimming pools, but not with puddles (Carey, 1978). And extension to non-concrete usages often occurs very late: 'I never heard of deep people anyway!'; 'No people are cold!' are typical responses of three- and four-year-olds when quizzed about abstract usages of words such as *deep* and *cold* (Asch & Nerlove, 1960). In summary, words are learned within particular contexts and are only gradually extended to their full range of meanings.

Underextension appears to characterise adult learning also. There are numerous words which an adult may use only within a particular context, sometimes even as a cliché, without fully understanding their meaning. *Chronic* might be actively applied only to ailments, such as *chronic catarrh*, *chronic indigestion*, and a phrase such as *chronic dislike* might initially cause bafflement. In language learning, then, full mastery normally follows on from previous usage within a limited context.

Overextensions are more noticeable, and so have been more frequently remarked upon. According to a once widespread view, they arise because a child 'perceives the world though a mental fog', and that at first 'rough classifications suffice' (Leopold, 1948, in Bar-Adon & Leopold, 1971: 99–101). This must be true to some extent, since the number of distinctions required is partly a matter of cultural convenience: English distinguishes between more types of dog than types of camel.

But the 'mental fog' viewpoint cannot account for apparently crazy categorisations, such as the child who used the word *moon* not only for the moon in all its phases, but also for various other non-moonlike objects, such as curved cow-horns, a slice of lemon and a shiny green leaf (Bowerman, 1980). Prototype theory provides a plausible explanation of such superficially weird overextensions (Bowerman, 1980; Griffiths, 1986). Arguably, the child has fastened on to a prototypical instance of the moon, perhaps a crescent moon in a picture book. Then, anything that shares a certain number of prototypical characteristics can be labelled 'moon': a full moon up in the sky, curved cow-horns which are seen from below, a pale yellow lemon slice, a green leaf which is curved and has the shininess associated with the moon. Such bizarre usages will gradually be dropped as the child readjusts its prototype to the adult one. But when the learning process is over, and the words are stored, they still have to be retrieved from the mental lexicon in order to be used.

Finding the Right Word

At one time, searching for a word was assumed to be like hunting for a required book in a library. A person went, metaphorically, to the shelf in the mental lexicon where it was stored, then pulled it out. If this selection took place in too much of a hurry, a neighbour might be accidentally picked, such as *left* instead of *right*, or *air-conditioner* instead of *refrigerator*. But this simple model is now thought to be unlikely (cf. Altmann & Shilcock, 1993; Levelt, 1993; Aitchison, 1994). Humans, it turns out, activate many more words than the one they actually require. The most direct evidence comes from blends, when two or more words are combined into one, as in *She* **chuttled** *at the news* (*chuckled* + *chortled*); *It's cold in* **Greeceland** (*Greenland* + *Iceland*, but said in a Greek restaurant).

Such examples indicate that the mind is subconsciously overpreparing itself, by activating numerous words. A similar conclusion can be drawn from speech errors such as *I bought eels and* **snake** (*skate*); *I'm waiting for the* **snow** *to melt* (*butter*, said while watching snow falling outside). In the first sentence, eels are sufficiently like snakes for *snake* to have been also activated, and the additional likeness of the word *skate* to *snake* caused *snake* to be actually uttered. In the second, an external observation activated the word *snow*, which found its way into the conversation in place of the required one. Such errors (alongside other evidence) suggest that it is normal to consider more words than are needed, and to suppress those which are unwanted.

An 'interactive activation' model may account for these phenomena, according to some recent research. This suggests that an initial impetus progressively fans out and spreads to more and more associated words. These connections involve both meaning and sound. A speaker seeking for the word *badger* might first activate the meaning of a number of woodland animals, such as 'rabbit', 'squirrel', 'badger', 'beaver'. Each of these would in turn activate a cluster of similar sound patterns. 'Rabbit' might activate *rabble, robot, rabbit*. 'Beaver' and 'badger' might each trigger *badger, beaker, beater, beaver*. Eventually, there will be dozens of different words in a state of excitation, all of which resemble the required word in either sound or meaning or both. The speaker will then have to suppress those which are not required. The exact mechanisms involved are still unclear. But in general, words that superficially fit both the sound and the meaning, such as *badger* and *beaver* in the example above, get progressively more aroused. Those that fail to fulfil both sound and meaning requirements, such as *robot* or *beaker*, fade away. Finally a winner will be selected, perhaps the wrong one if there are two similar candidates, as in *beaver* and *badger*.

At least superficially, these interactive activation models tie in with current ideas about how the brain works. For most of the past ten years or so, standard digital computers have been the major metaphor for human language processes, yet this analogy has not proved particularly fruitful. Now the situation is reversed; the brain is being taken as a source of inspiration for the new mental models: 'We wish to replace the "computer metaphor" as a model of the mind with the "brain metaphor" as a model of the mind' (Rumelhart, Hinton & McClelland, 1986: 75). Massive parallel processing is regarded as inevitable. Furthermore, the connections between units are of greater importance than their absolute locations, which may be widely distributed. For this reason, these models are known by the generic names of either 'connectionist' models or 'parallel distributed processing' (PDP) models.

Such models shed new light on the old controversy about the relationship between different languages in the mind. Connectionist models suggest that all lexical items from every language are potentially interconnected. Discussion of an owl in one language would subconsciously trigger the word for 'owl' in any other language known to the speaker. Someone who is totally fluent in a language will be able to suppress the unwanted owl words, but if he or she is not in full control, then the unwanted words — probably those from their own native language — are likely to distract attention and make it impossible to think of the required one (Green, 1986).

It is not yet clear how the insights derived from these new theories of word retrieval can be applied to teaching and translating, but as the processes involved are clarified, the easier it will be to prepare training schemes which are consistent with these findings, or, perhaps more importantly, avoid devising programmes which go against the 'natural' way of doing things.

Conclusion

This paper has tried to give an overview of some recent findings on the mental lexicon which have implications for those actively involved in learning, teaching or translating vocabulary. The following points have been mentioned as likely to be of interest:

(1) The mental lexicon is much larger than many people have assumed. Educated native speakers of English can probably understand and potentially use at least 50,000 lexical items.

(2) Humans work from prototypes: they rank items within categories, with some examples being regarded as prototypical and others as less good. These rankings vary across cultures. Category borderlines also differ from language to language.

(3) In the mental lexicon the strongest connections are possibly collocational links and links between coordinates.

(4) In vocabulary acquisition, underextensions are more frequent than overextensions. Apparently strange overextensions can sometimes be explained by a learner's selection of an idiosyncratic prototype.

(5) In word retrieval, humans activate more words than are required and then suppress the unwanted ones.

The plethora of recent findings on the lexicon suggests that it is at last beginning to acquire the prominence within linguistics, psycholinguistics and applied linguistics that it deserves. Finally, researchers are realising that words are not just isolated trivia but part of a complex interlocking system, whose acquisition is fairly amazing. As two researchers note:

> The ability of children to conform to the grammatical rules is only slightly more wonderful than their ability to learn new words... What one tends to overlook is the sheer magnitude of the child's achievement. Simply learning the vocabulary is an enormous undertaking. (Miller & Gildea, 1987: 86)

At last, we may be on the way to an understanding of this mammoth achievement.

Notes

1. The points outlined in this chapter are discussed in Aitchison (1994). This chapter, when first presented as a paper, was intended to highlight parts of this book as of special interest for those involved in translation and language teaching/learning.

References

AITCHISON, J. 1992a, Good birds, better birds and amazing birds. In P.J.L. ARNAUD and H. BEJOINT (eds) *Vocabulary and Applied Linguistics* (pp. 71–84). London: Macmillan.
— 1992b, Chains, nets and boxes: The linguistic capture of love, anger and fear. In W.G. BUSSE (ed.) *Anglistentag 1991 Düsseldorf, Proceedings*. Berlin: Mouton de Gruyter.
— 1994, *Words in the Mind: An Introduction to the Mental Lexicon* 2nd edn. Oxford: Blackwell.
AITCHISON, J. and KOPPEL, A. 1990, *The Lexicon in 11–14-year-olds: LSE-Longman Project*. (Mimeo).
ALTMAN, G.T.M. and SHILCOCK, R. 1993, *Cognitive Models of Speech Processing*. Hove: Lawrence Erlbaum.
ASCH, S.E. and NERLOVE, H. 1960, The development of double-function terms in children: An exploratory investigation. In B. KAPLAN and S. WAPNER (eds) *Perspectives in Psychological Theory* (pp. 47–60). New York: International Universities Press.
BAR-ADON, A. and LEOPOLD, W.F. 1971, *Child Language: A Book of Readings*. Englewood Cliffs, NJ: Prentice-Hall.
BOWERMAN, M. 1980, The structure and origin of semantic categories in the language learning child. In D. FOSTER and S. BRANDES (eds) *Symbol as Sense: New Approaches to the Analysis of Meaning* (pp. 277–99). New York: Academic Press.
BUTTERWORTH, B., HOWARD, D. and McLOUGHLIN, P. 1984, The semantic deficit in aphasia: The relationship between semantic errors in auditory comprehension and picture naming. *Neuropsychologia* 22, 409–26.
CAREY, S. 1978, The child as word learner. In M. HALLE, J. BRESNAN and G.A. MILLER (eds) *Linguistic Theory and Psychological Reality* (pp. 264–93). Cambridge, MA: MIT Press.
CLARK, E.V. 1993, *The Lexicon in Acquisition*. Cambridge: Cambridge University Press.
CRUSE, D.A. 1986, *Lexical Semantics*. Cambridge: Cambridge University Press.
FARRAR, F.W. 1865, *Chapters on Language*. London: Longmans Green.
GEERAERTS, D. 1989, Prospects and problems of prototype theory. *Linguistics* 27, 587–612.
GREEN, D. 1986, Control, activation and resource: A framework and model for the control of speech in bilinguals. *Brain and Language* 27, 210–23.
GREEN, J. 1982, *A Dictionary of Contemporary Quotations*. London: Pan Books.
GRIFFITHS, P. 1986, Early vocabulary. In P. FLETCHER and M. GARMAN (eds) *Language Acquisition*, 2nd edn (pp. 279–306). Cambridge: Cambridge University Press.

HART, J., BERNDT, R.S. and CARAMAZZA, A. 1985, Category-specific naming deficit following cerebral infarction. *Nature* 316, 439–40.
KATZ, J.J. and FODOR, J.A. 1963, The structure of a semantic theory. *Language* 39, 170–210.
LABOV, W. 1973, The boundaries of words and their meanings. In C-J. N. BAILEY and R. W. SHUY (eds) *New Ways of Analyzing Variation in English* (pp. 340–73). Washington, DC: Georgetown University Press.
LAKOFF, G. 1972, Hedges: A study in meaning criteria and the logic of fuzzy concepts. *Papers of the Eighth Regional Meeting, Chicago Linguistic Society*, 183–228.
LAKOFF, G. 1987, *Women, Fire and Dangerous Things*. Chicago, IL: Chicago University Press.
LEHRER, A. and KITTAY, E.F. 1992, *Frames, Fields and Contrasts*. Hillsdale, NJ: Lawrence Erlbaum.
LEVELT, W.J.M. 1993, *Lexical Access in Speech Production*. Oxford: Basil Blackwell.
LEVIN, B. and PINKER, S. 1992, *Lexical and Conceptual Semantics*. Oxford: Basil Blackwell.
LIVELY, P. 1987/1988, *Moon Tiger*. Harmondsworth: Penguin.
MILLER, G.A. 1990, WordNet: An online lexical database. *International Journal of Lexicography*, Special issue, 3 (4).
MILLER, G. A. and GILDEA, P.M. 1987, How children learn words. *Scientific American* 257, 86–91.
ROSCH, E. 1975, Cognitive representations of semantic categories. *Journal of Experimental Psychology: General* 104, 192–233.
RUMELHART, D.E., HINTON, G.E. and McCLELLAND, J.L. 1986, A general framework for parallel distributed processing. In D. E. RUMELHART and J. L. McCLELLAND (eds) *Parallel Distributed Processing: Explorations in the Microstructure of Cognition*, vol. 1 (pp.45–76). Cambridge, MA: MIT Press.
TAYLOR, J.R. 1989, *Linguistic Categorisation: Prototypes in Linguistic Theory*. Oxford: Clarendon Press.
WARRINGTON, E.K. 1981, Neuropsychological studies of verbal semantic systems. *Philosophical Transactions of the Royal Society of London* B 295, 411–23.
WIERZBICKA, A. 1992, *Semantics, Culture and Cognition*. Oxford: Oxford University Press.
WITTGENSTEIN, L. 1958, *Philosophical Investigations* 2nd edn. Trans. G.E.M. Anscombe. Oxford: Basil Blackwell.

3 The Classical Research in L2 Vocabulary Acquisition

PAUL MEARA

A few years ago it was fashionable to describe vocabulary acquisition as a neglected aspect of language learning. Recently, however, interest in this area has unexpectedly grown at an enormous rate. There seems to be a general feeling among teachers, publishers and researchers that vocabulary acquisition has not been treated seriously enough in the past, and that our beliefs about how people acquire vocabulary in a foreign language are due for overhaul. At times like this, what generally happens is that people working in the field rediscover work that was carried out many years before. Papers which have remained in peaceful obscurity for many years suddenly start to be quoted in bibliographies, and become part of the collective folklore. Since 1980 or so, this tendency has become increasingly apparent in current research on vocabulary acquisition.

This chapter presents a summary of 'major' empirical research on vocabulary acquisition carried out between 1900 and 1960. It is not a definitive survey, because such a survey would be beyond the scope of a chapter of this length. My working definition of 'major' is any empirical study which has been cited at least twice in the current literature (i.e. since 1980) as part of a theoretical argument about vocabulary acquisition. This literature is comprehensively reviewed in Meara (1987, 1992). This criterion gives us a set of 13 papers. The chapter provides a summary of all this work, and a critical analysis of some of the issues these studies point to. I hope that my reading of this research might highlight some areas in which these experiments need to be treated with caution, and how some of the more obvious misinterpretations might be avoided.

The papers to be discussed are summarised in Tables 3.1 and 3.2. Table 3.1 identifies the author(s) and date of each paper, the type and number of subjects who took part in each experiment, the language of the stimuli, and the number of words the subjects were required to learn. Table 3.2 reports the type of experimental task used to measure acquisition and a brief summary of the findings.

Discussion

Although these experiments deal with a number of quite different aspects of vocabulary acquisition, there are a few common themes that deserve comment. These are, at the simplest level: subjects, languages, target language (TL) words to be learned, and the tasks used to assess learning; at a more complex level, the important issue seems to be the role that models play in research.

Table 3.1 Major studies in vocabulary acquisition: basic materials

Author(s)	Subjects	Language	Target Words
1. Thorndike 1914	28 adults: b	German & nonsense	4 * 20
2. Grinstead 1915	1 adult	German	(300+)
3. Seibert 1927	81 students	French	(3 * 30)
4. Anderson & Jordan 1928	31 children: b	Latin	(10 * 25)
5. Stoddard 1929	328 children: b	French	2 * 25
6. Seibert 1930	60 adults	French	12
7. Chapman & Gilbert 1937	121 children: b	Hindustani	48
8. Forlano & Hoffman 1937	65 children: b	Hebrew	2 * 20
9. Morgan & Bailey 1943	84 adults: b	Ru-ro	(120)
10. Morgan & Bonham 1944	148 children: b	Ru-ro	(6 * 20)
11. Morgan & Foltz 1944	58 children: b	French	(100)
12. Kopstein & Roshal 1954	788 adults: b	Russian	8
13. Kopstein & Roshal 1955	96 'groups': b	(Russian)	8

(Details in parentheses are inferred from the text.)
: b indicates that the subjects were absolute beginners.

L2 VOCABULARY ACQUISITION

Table 3.2 Methods and Results

1. Thorndike compared two ways of learning words in listed pairs: (a) the repetition method, where each list is simply read aloud until learning is achieved, and (b) the recall method, where the list is read through once, and the subject then covers up one member of each pair and guesses the other. Thorndike recorded the time taken to learn the lists and the number of correct responses on a test. Repetition is faster and produces slightly better test results, but these differences are not significant.

2. Grinstead compared (a) learning words from context with (b) learning words from lists. In (a) the single subject read a text and listed any unknown words. In (b) a list of words was presented and the subject deleted from this list any words he already knew. The unknown words were then looked up in a dictionary and later retention of their meanings was tested. Method (a) produces a small advantage over (b).

3. Seibert compared three ways of learning word lists: (a) silent learning, (b) learning aloud and (c) learning aloud accompanied by an immediate written recall of the words learned. In all methods Seibert required subjects to learn the lists by rote, and the time necessary for this was roughly recorded. All subjects performed each task over an extended period; relearning trials and tests were administered after 2, 10 and 42 days. Seibert claims that methods (b) and (c) produce fastest relearning, and that accuracy was greatest when items were learned aloud.

4. Anderson and Jordan taught sets of different types of Latin words to 12-year-old children, and looked at rates of learning and forgetting. Words were learned in lists of about 25 words, one list a day, with 15 seconds allowed for each word. Learning was measured by a recognition test. The authors report that cognate words are learned better than non-cognates or semi-cognate words, and that single words are learned better than phrases. About half the items learned are still retained after two months, but cognate and semi-cognate words hold up best; these stimuli produce a shallow U-shaped forgetting curve. Children who learn lots of words retain them better than those who learn fewer words.

Table 3.2 (*cont.*)

5 Stoddard compared the learning of word lists presented as (a) English–French pairs or as (b) French–English pairs. 20 minutes was allowed for the entire task. Subsequent testing showed that French–English order produced better learning.

6 Seibert compared acquisition of vocabulary in (a) paired associate lists, (b) in sentence contexts, and (c) in a combination of both of these. Recall was tested after 50 minutes, 2 days, 15 days and 40 days. Seibert reports that (a) is consistently superior to the other methods, and that this superiority is maintained over the 40-day test period. (Cf. also Seibert, 1945)

7 Chapman and Gilbert tested the claim that it is easier to learn a foreign language word if you also know what the word means in your native language: i.e. if you do not know the meaning of *tompion*[1] in English, learning its Russian translation will be hard. The authors paired known and unknown words with random Hindustani words, and taught these pairs to the children by running through the entire list in a number of successive presentations, with a test after each run. Results, not surprisingly, showed that known words always produced better learning than unknown words, and that the familiar words are less likely to be forgotten.

8 Forlano and Hoffman compared two methods of teaching word lists. In the telling method, each word is read aloud by the teacher and the children are then told what it means; in the guessing method, each word is read aloud and the children have to guess its meaning. They are then told the true meaning, and correct their guess if it was wrong. Retention of meaning was tested immediately after learning, and again after two days. The telling method produces better learning.

9 Morgan and Bailey used a set of artificial stimuli based on French to test the claim that words could be learned effectively in context. Subjects were provided with either (a) a simple story, or (b) a set of decontextualised materials. Both groups were provided with a dictionary and asked to produce a translation of their material. They were later tested on their ability to produce English translations given the Ru-ro word forms. The results failed to show any significant differences due to the type of material studied.

Table 3.2 (*cont.*)

10 Morgan and Bonham investigated the effects of part of speech on vocabulary acquisition, by requiring learners to learn lists of 20 word pairs in English and Ru-ro. The lists contained three nouns, three pronouns, three verbs, three adjectives, three adverbs, three prepositions and two interjections. Each word pair was exposed for 1.5 seconds, and after all 20 words had been seen, a test was administered. This procedure was repeated until all 20 words could be recognised three times in succession. The number of exposures required by each word was recorded. Significant differences between word types were found: nouns were easiest, adverbs hardest.

11 Morgan and Foltz's experiment is a replication of Morgan and Bailey's, but using French words in place of Ru-ro. Results showed no significant differences between groups.

12 Kopstein and Roshal compared teaching words (a) with pictures and (b) in printed form. A recognition test was used to assess learning. Better learning was found with (a).

13 Kopstein and Roshal compared two methods of teaching foreign words. In (a) the foreign word and the English word were displayed simultaneously for 3.5 seconds; in (b) the foreign word was displayed for two seconds and then simultaneously with the English word for 1.5 seconds. Method (a) was very much better than method (b) at first, but the difference disappeared as more substantial levels of learning were reached.

Subjects

A glance at Table 3.1 reveals that there is an enormous discrepancy in the number of subjects taking part in these experiments. Such discrepancies are not peculiar to vocabulary studies, of course, but they are fairly important in this area, since we know that there are very large individual differences in the way people handle words (cf. for example, Hunt, 1978). In the studies I have listed the number of subjects ranges from Grinstead's single subject to Kopstein and Roshal's 788. None of the papers gives any explanation for the number of subjects used, and there is clearly a general feeling that the number is arbitrary as long as it is obviously sufficient. This is a rather surprising conclusion. Ideally, what is required is a number big enough to iron out the variation due to individual differences, but ironically, in these studies the experiments with the largest number of subjects make no attempt to control for extraneous variables that might affect vocabulary uptake. Stoddard, for example, mentions that his subjects produced huge amounts of variation, their scores ranging from 2 to 50 items on a 50-item test, but he does not attempt to explore the sources of this difference.

A second, but in some ways more important problem is that in most of the experiments the subjects are naive, in the sense that their prior experience of the language they were supposed to be learning was nil. This is an important limitation, because it means that these experiments deal in effect only with the very earliest stages of learning a language. It could be argued that acquiring a few words in a language that you are wholly ignorant of, is quite different from acquiring the same number of words in a language you know moderately well. In these later stages a learner will already have developed a good feel for the formal aspects of words in the TL. This should reduce the learning burden considerably and make it easier to acquire the TL words, the more proficient the learner is. At the same time, morphological information and comparisons with known words of similar meaning should also make it easier to fix the meaning and form of a TL word. Considerations of this sort obviously restrict the way the results reported here can be applied to other types of learner. In effect, only three of these studies dealt with non-beginners, and of these the two studies by Seibert deal with '81 students who had the equivalent of one year of college work in French' (Seibert, 1927: 296) and 'sixty college students in second year French' (Seibert, 1930: 299).

It is not very clear what sort of level this description represents, but it is probably fair to guess that it is not very advanced. This leaves Grinstead's study as the only one which reports on the behaviour of advanced subjects, and this study deals with only a single individual. The limitations of this database are very clear, and it is obviously going to be very difficult to make statements about 'vocabulary acquisition' in general on the strength of these reports.

Languages

The same sort of limitation is also apparent in the range of languages studied in these experiments. A number of the studies use TLs which are totally artificial. Morgan and Bailey's Ru-ro consisted of 114 artificial words with a syntax that was an exact parallel of French. Chapman and Gilbert technically used Hindustani, but in fact they merely gave their children lists of English words paired randomly with Hindustani words; the word pairs were *not* translations. Forlano and Hoffman used Hebrew words and their English translations. The remaining studies use TL words from four closely-related Indo-European languages. In spite of these restrictions, all the authors make a point of extrapolating from their rather limited data to general, universal statements about learning foreign vocabularies. This is an important simplification, because it ignores the fact that different types of language present quite different learning problems to individual learners.

Take, for instance, the cases of a Dutch speaker, a Spanish speaker, an Arab and a Vietnamese learning English. By and large, the Dutch speaker will find basic English vocabulary easy, since most of it is cognate with items in the L1. There might be problems with less frequent vocabulary, but by the time this has been reached, the learner probably has a high level of independence and autonomy anyway. In contrast, a Spanish speaker will generally find basic English vocabulary difficult: it is structurally very different from basic vocabulary in Spanish, and there are few cognates. However, Spanish speakers have a huge latent vocabulary of low-frequency English words which are cognate with Spanish items, and this should mean that their ability to acquire new words improves dramatically with their general level of competence in English (cf. also Anderman and Rogers, this volume, for the relevance of cognates in language learning for translators). The Arab and the Vietnamese speakers have no such help from their L1, and the process of acquiring new words will never get any easier for them. At the same time, however, these two learners will find English vocabulary difficult in different ways because of the way their L1 lexicons are shaped and structured.

Words to be learned

Just as we saw that there was a discrepancy in the number of subjects used in the experiments, there is a similar discrepancy in the number of words to be learned. The figures here range from Kopstein and Roshal's amazingly low figure of eight words to Grinstead's more ambitious target of 300 plus. Most of the studies cluster in the 20–40 word range, although sometimes the subjects are asked to learn a number of lists of this length. Again, however, there is no justification for why these figures are chosen, or whether such a figure is an appropriate one. The basic problem is that all the authors are assuming it is possible to model the acquisition of an entire vocabulary by looking at how effectively a tiny subset of this vocabulary is acquired in tightly-controlled conditions.

There are a number of obvious reasons why this position is untenable. First, learning a set of 20–40 words may pose some difficulties for short-term memory, but seen from a long-term perspective, and in comparison with the number of words a fluent speaker needs to know (cf. Aitchison, this volume), such numbers are basically trivial. Many people can handle a vocabulary of a few tens of words by using simple mnemonic techniques, for example. It is not obvious, however, that these techniques would enable a learner to handle, say, 2,000 new words — the number of words needed to handle about 80% of English text. Secondly, and more importantly, a vocabulary of 30–40 words can be efficiently handled by treating it as an unconnected list of discrete items. Bigger vocabularies, on the other hand, will contain subsets of words which are linked together on either semantic or morphological grounds, and these linkages must make it inefficient to treat the vocabulary as a simple list. At the very least, some sort of network structure must develop in a large vocabulary which reflects these relationships between the component items of the total vocabulary. Presumably, what makes it difficult to acquire a large vocabulary is that it takes time and effort for these connections to develop, and for a properly organised lexicon to emerge. This problem does not arise when the target lexicon contains only a handful of words.

Learning methods

The studies we have been discussing make use of a highly-restricted set of learning methods. Most of them use the time-honoured method of learning the TL words in lists, paired off with their L1 translations, and there are a number of variations on this theme. In most cases, however, the method is treated in a rather rigid fashion: what is measured is the number of trials, or the total time required to learn the entire list of words, so that the learners are allowed no flexibility in their learning. Anderson and Jordan's 15 seconds per word is a good example of this approach. The other method used is to present words in contexts, but apart from Grinstead's real-life contexts, the studies reported here all used highly artificial contexts. In addition, since most of the learners were absolute beginners, it is difficult to see why the contexts might be expected to help very much in any case. Morgan and Bailey's contexts, for example, consisted of a story made up of 114 totally unknown words in a language whose syntactic structure was also unknown. This means that the new words may have been related to each other through the situations described, but it is hard to imagine that this context could provide any real support to the learner, and it is not really surprising, therefore, that Morgan and Bailey failed to find any significant differences in their study.

It is easy to explain this concentration on lists of isolated words in historical terms, but the use of a single presentation method limits this research in a very basic way. There are two reasons for this. First, we know from studies of 'good language learners' that effective study of vocabulary often involves the use of many different learning methods (cf. for example, Naiman et al., 1975). Good learners rarely rely on list learning as a way of increasing their vocabulary; rather, they actively seek out new words and incorporate them into their personal word stock using a variety of learning techniques. The second reason why list learning is unsatisfactory is that, although it may be effective for small numbers of words, it is much less obviously effective as a way a learning large vocabularies. In these experiments, for example, Stoddard allowed his subjects 20 minutes to learn 25 words, i.e. roughly one word per minute. Even with this generous time allowance, and with a fairly loose set of criteria for accepting a word as acquired, Stoddard's subjects managed to acquire only 15 words. If you allow for subsequent forgetting of a proportion of these words, say 50%, then the effective learning rate is something like three minutes per word. At this rate it would take 50 hours of study time to acquire a vocabulary of 1,000 words — not a great deal of time objectively, perhaps, but a very long time when judged against the amount of time typically available to language learners. Experiments that are restricted to the learning of very small numbers of words clearly mask this basic problem.

Assessment

Much the same criticisms can be made of the way in which the subjects' grasp of the vocabulary was tested in these experiments. All the studies reported simply ask for the TL word to be translated into English, and this means that even in the experiments where words were initially learned in context, only the ability to recognise decontextualised words was measured. It is not obvious to me that this measure is a good test of how well vocabulary items have been learned. At best it tests passive recognition skills rather than active acquisition of items; at worst it tests passive recognition of one item out of a set which has only just been studied — this means that recognition of any characteristic which distinguishes the word from the rest of the set would be enough to give a correct answer. Testing in this way gives no indication of whether a particular word can be put to active use, or whether some partial knowledge might have been acquired which could facilitate learning in future encounters. Furthermore, this kind of testing gives no indication of how resistant the word might be to forgetting or to confusion with other words, both problems which increase as the number of words to be learned gets larger.

Conclusion

Although I have been ostensibly discussing work on vocabulary acquisition carried out some 30 or 40 years ago, readers who are familiar with the contemporary literature will recognise that many of the comments I have made apply equally well to work that has appeared more recently (cf. Meara, 1983, 1987, 1992). In some ways, we seem to have made very little real progress since Grinstead. None of the questions asked by the researchers listed in Table 3.1 has been definitively resolved, and it is perhaps worthwhile asking why there is so little sign that any of the work carried out since 1960 has had any serious impact on course design or teaching practice.

My own view is that a lot of current research is making the same mistakes that can be found in the earlier work on vocabulary acquisition. The main problem areas noted in the early work are still apparent today. The first, and perhaps the most important of these is that none of us has any idea of the extent to which individual differences affect vocabulary acquisition, though we do know that individual differences in L1 vocabulary skills are very large indeed. This means that we still do not have a motivated reason for using experimental groups of a particular size, and we do not know how far our results are generalisable to wider populations. A recent collection of studies on 'the use and acquisition of the second language lexicon' (Gass, 1987), which I will take as representative of current experimental practice, includes seven papers, where the number of subjects ranges from 15 to 244. Again, there is no principled explanation for these numbers apart from availability, and one is left wondering whether it is really necessary to do experiments with 244 subjects in one condition, and just how much variation you would expect to find in a group as large as this. Conversely, one might ask whether a group of 26 subjects comprising 5 Arabic speakers, 1 Chinese, 1 Farsi speaker, 1 Greek, 1 'Indonesian', 5 Japanese, 1 Portuguese, 9 Spanish speakers, 1 Thai and 1 Turk can really be considered representative of anything at all (Ard & Gass, 1987). The short answer to this question is that we do not know, of course. There is, however, plenty of evidence that vocabulary-handling skills in L1 vary enormously, and it seems very likely that the same sort of variation will apply in the case of L2 learners. However, until we know the extent of this variation, and how it is made up, we are unlikely to come up with convincing models of how vocabularies are acquired. It seems to me that the question of how much individual variation there is in vocabulary skills really needs to be made a top priority in L2 vocabulary acquisition research.

The second problem area is that most of the current research still looks at a very restricted range of languages, and generalises from this narrow base to vocabulary acquisition in general. As in the case of the early research, almost all the current work is based on Indo-European languages, despite the fact that cognate vocabularies seem relatively easy to learn and that non-Indo-European languages are known to cause special problems in the area of vocabulary acquisition. As an example, consider Gass's (1987) collection again. Here, the seven papers cover French and English bilinguals, Dutch learners of English, Swedish learners of English, and groups of mixed subjects learning English or learning Hebrew — if anything, a rather narrower spread of languages than was found in the classical research, with a heavy emphasis on the acquisition of English as an L2. This narrow spread in itself is not a problem, but the concentration on the acquisition of English must distort the field. English vocabulary is very peculiar: it seems to be inordinately large compared to the basic vocabularies of other languages, for instance (cf. Newmark, this volume for a discussion of this with respect to translation) and, compared to other languages, English seems to rely less on systematic combinations of items, and rather more on discrete items. In terms of Cruttenden's distinction between items and system, English seems to have more items and less system than many other languages do (cf. Ringbom, 1983).

There are, in fact, very few studies which make comparisons between learners from different backgrounds acquiring the same L2, and very few studies of learners from the same L1 background acquiring different L2s. To my knowledge, there is, for example, no work on the acquisition of Chinese or Arabic vocabularies by English speakers, and only a handful of papers on the acquisition of English vocabulary by native speakers of non-Indo-European languages. There are two notable exceptions to this claim. A series of studies comparing the English vocabulary of Finns and Swedes shows without exception that Finns have to work much harder at acquiring English vocabulary than Swedish speakers do (cf. Takala, 1984; Ringbom, 1987). There is also a major cross-linguistic study of migrant L2 learners, where systematic comparisons between learners from the same L1 background acquiring different L2s were carried out (Broeder et al., 1988). This work is difficult to evaluate because the number of subjects in each comparison group is tiny (usually three), and this takes us back to the question of individual differences and variation at the lexical level.

What we really need, then, is a systematic programme of replications, where studies carried out with small, homogenous groups of learners are repeated with other groups with different characteristics. At the moment, there is no sign of a systematic programme of this sort.

The third similarity between current work and the early research is a general assumption that acquiring words in an L2 is basically the same process, regardless of the stage the learner is at. A great deal of current research deals with volunteer subjects who learn a set of words in laboratory experiments, and who are therefore effectively absolute beginners. Rather more work on advanced learners is being carried out, but this work still concentrates on how well a particular set of words is acquired by learners at a given level of proficiency. Few, if any attempts have been made to assess how the overall structure of the L2 lexicon develops, or how the size of a learner's lexicon affects the way new words are acquired. It is easy to see why this should be, of course. There are no obvious ways of describing complexity in the lexicon, or how a small lexicon differs from a large one (other than by its size). It is much easier to think of the lexicon as an unstructured list of words, rather than as a complex, interlocking structure (cf. Aitchison, this volume, on the organisation of the mental lexicon). This is clearly a problem that we will have to address if we are to understand what is really going on in a developing lexicon.

Finally, we still do not seem to have made any real advances in the measurement of vocabulary acquisition. A number of more recent papers (notably Richards, 1976) have discussed what 'knowing a word' means. Unfortunately, these discussions have not yet led to any working models or tests which might be used in psycholinguistic experiments, and most of the current research still looks at vocabulary as discrete items which can be marked correct or incorrect on the basis of simple recognition or production tests. The simple binary model which underlies these tests is a very crude one; it does not accord well with most learners' personal experience and it seems inherently incapable of allowing us to develop a sensitive model of what learning words in an L2 really involves.

At the same time, the modern literature on vocabulary acquisition includes a huge number of different experimental tasks: lexical decision tasks, word association tasks, sentence completion tasks, and so on. In theory this diversity should allow us to 'triangulate' on the really important issues in vocabulary acquisition. In practice, it seems to me that it contributes to a serious fragmentation of the field. There are too few of us working in this area to explore fully what each of these different techniques does. The data each of us produces is often quite incompatible with data other people produce, and this makes it very difficult to put all our findings together into a single coherent picture.

A solution to both these problems might be found if we could develop a series of standardised tasks, or agreed 'benchmarks' which we could use to assess the acquisition of words. It ought to be relatively easy to agree on what these benchmarks should be. They would need to be technologically simple; they would have to be usable with learners from different L1 backgrounds, and usable with learners at different levels of proficiency; but, at the same time they would need to be sufficiently rich and sensitive to reflect the richness of the real world. In short, a challenging combination of real-world constraints and rich theory. This may sound like a tall order, but if we cannot develop standard, reliable tools of this sort, then in the long run we will continue to produce data whose relevance is strictly limited. Until we begin to tackle these problems systematically, we are likely to continue covering much the same ground as the classical researchers did, and with equally unconvincing results.

Acknowledgements

Thanks to Angela Lilley, Sue Gass and Jan-Arjen Mondria, who provided detailed comments on earlier drafts of this chapter.

Notes

1. Tompion — 'a small pellet of mud and saliva which a bear inserts in its anus before hibernating for the winter to stop the ants getting in'.

References

ANDERSON, J. and JORDAN, A. 1928, Learning and retention of Latin words and phrases. *Journal of Educational Psychology* 19, 485–96.
ARD, J. and GASS, S. 1987, Lexical constraints on syntactic acquisition. In S. GASS (ed.) *The Use and Acquisition of the Second Language Lexicon.* Special Issue, *Studies in Second Language Acquisition* 9, 2, 233–51.
BROEDER, P., EXTRA, G., HOUT, R. VAN, STRÖMQVIST, S. and VOIONMAA, K. 1988, *Processes in the Developing Lexicon.* Tilburg.
CHAPMAN, I. and GILBERT, L. 1937, A study of the influence of familiarity with English words upon the learning of their foreign language equivalents. *Journal of Educational Psychology* 28, 621–8.
FORLANO, G. and HOFFMAN, M. 1937, Guessing and telling methods in learning words in a foreign language. *Journal of Educational Psychology* 28, 632–6.
GASS, S. (ed.) 1987, *The Use and Acquisition of the Second Language Lexicon.* Special Issue, *Studies in Second Language Acquisition* 9, 2.
GRINSTEAD, W. 1915, An experiment in the learning of foreign words. *American Psychologist* 9, 407–8.
HUNT, E. 1978, The mechanics of verbal ability. *Psychological Review* 85, 109–30.
KOPSTEIN, F. and ROSHAL, S. 1954, Learning foreign vocabulary from pictures vs. words. *American Psychologist* 9, 407–8.
— 1955, Method of presenting word pairs as a factor in foreign vocabulary learning. *American Psychologist* 10, 354.

MEARA, P. 1983, *Vocabulary in a Second Language*. London: Centre for Information on Language Teaching.
— 1987, *Vocabulary in a Second Language* Vol. 2. London: Centre for Information on Language Teaching.
— 1992, Vocabulary in a Second Language Vol. 3. *Reading in a Foreign Language* 9, 761–837.
MORGAN, C. and BAILEY, D. 1943, The effect of context on learning vocabulary. *Journal of Educational Psychology* 34, 561–5.
MORGAN, C.L. and BONHAM, D.N. 1944, Difficulty of vocabulary learning as affected by parts of speech. *Journal of Educational Psychology* 35, 369–77.
MORGAN, C. and FOLTZ, M. 1944, The effect of context on learning a French vocabulary. *Journal of Educational Research* 38, 213–6.
NAIMAN, N., FRÖLICH, M., STERN, H. and TEDESCO, A. 1975, *The Good Language Learner*. Toronto: Ontario Institute for Studies in Education.
RICHARDS, J. 1976, The role of vocabulary teaching. *TESOL Quarterly* 10, 77–89.
RINGBOM, H. 1983, On the distinction of item learning vs. system learning and receptive competence vs. productive competence in relation to the role of L1 in foreign language learning. In H. RINGBOM (ed) *Psycholinguistics and Foreign Language Learning* (pp.163–73). Åbo: Åbo Akademi.
— 1987, *The Role of the First Language in Foreign Language Learning*. Clevedon: Multilingual Matters.
SEIBERT, L. 1927, An experiment in learning French vocabulary. *Journal of Educational Psychology* 18, 294–309.
— 1930, An experiment on the relative efficiency of studying French in associated pairs vs. studying French words in context. *Journal of Educational Psychology* 21, 297–314.
— 1945, An experiment on the practice of guessing word meanings from context. *Modern Languages Journal* 29, 305–14.
STODDARD, G. 1929, An experiment in verbal learning. *Journal of Educational Psychology* 20, 452–7.
TAKALA, S. 1984, *Evaluation of Students' Knowledge of English Vocabulary in the Finnish Comprehensive School*. Jyväskylä: Jyväskylän Yliopisto.
THORNDIKE, E. 1914, Repetition versus recall in memorising vocabularies. *Journal of Educational Psychology* 5, 596–7.

4 The Word is My Oyster — The Language Learner and the Translator

GUNILLA ANDERMAN

The role of 'prototype theory' in the learning of new words in L1 as well as in L2 acquisition is of interest to anyone working with vocabulary and word meaning. With respect to L1 acquisition, there is evidence to suggest that children may be working from prototypes when they first try to decide on the meaning of new words, trying to match them against the prototype of the relevant category (Aitchison, 1992, 1994). Some interesting observations have also been made with respect to 'prototype effect' in relation to language acquisition among L2 learners (Viberg, 1985, 1988; Kotsinas, 1985). In addition, 'prototypology' has become a useful notion in the now burgeoning field of translation studies, particularly in discussions of the difficulties involved in establishing equivalence between source language (SL) and target language (TL) (Neubert & Shreve, 1993; Snell-Hornby, 1993). Thus far, however, few attempts, if any, appear to have been made to bring together the observations related to prototype theory in all three areas of research in order to establish the extent to which translation studies may benefit from the findings already made within the fields of L1 and L2 acquisition.

The purpose of this chapter is to look at some of the relevant findings in the study of L1 and L2 acquisition and to discuss their implications for the field of translation studies. It starts by discussing the notion of prototype and the main tenets of so-called prototype theory. This is followed by a discussion of its applicability to L1 and L2 acquisition. The findings of cross-linguistic research in these fields are then applied to translation. The concluding section discusses ongoing work in the field of translation studies, concerned with prototypology, and brief mention is made of an offshoot of prototype theory (cf. Aitchison, this volume), also of potential interest to the translator.

Prototype Theory

From an early age children seem to be able to sort objects into basic-level categories such as *cat* and *dog*, and these also appear to be the categories which are most likely to be learnt first (Berlin, 1978). Work on categorisation has also shown that among the members of these categories there are some which seem to be perceived by speakers as more 'typical' than others (Rosch, 1973, 1975; Rosch & Lloyd, 1978). There was significant agreement, for instance, among English-speaking interviewees that an apple is a better example of a fruit than an olive, and that a car made a better vehicle than a scooter (Rosch, 1973).

In a differentiated system the core or basic level appears to be a natural point of entry in our pursuit of new knowledge. It also appears to be the level of categorisation that the small child can master at an early age, whereas categorisation on the superordinate level (animal, in the case of cat and dog) or on the subordinate level (bulldog, dachshund, Burmese, Siamese) presents considerably greater difficulties. Not surprisingly, this basic level is also the heart of Linnaeus's system of taxonomic classification of plants. Here it is known as the genus, the level of general characteristics, while the species is defined in terms of differentiating features.

However, the particular characteristics that may be distinguished on this basic level, where most of our knowledge appears to be organised, are defined by the perceptual systems of those who do the distinguishing. While adults may agree on what they consider to be typical features of people, objects or actions, children — with much more limited experience of the world around them — might focus on different distinguishable characteristics and, as a result, analyse the prototype differently. In fact, it seems to take a long time for learners to become fully aware of adult native speakers' treatment of categories, a knowledge they may not necessarily acquire until adolescence (Aitchison, 1992: 78). Looked at in this light, child and adult language might be viewed as being different simply as the result of differences in the analysis given to the prototype.

First Language Acquisition

With respect to L1 acquisition, the literature seems to abound in reports of early and erroneous stabs at classification by very young children. As early as 1906, Major observed that his two-year-old son first used the word *mum* about horses, and then overextended its use to include a number of other animals. In order to ascertain the true nature of a *mum*, Major took his son on a visit to the zoo. It turned out that the boy used *mum* for a number of animals he had not seen before, including a hippopotamus, an opossum, a tiger and a wolf, while he referred to monkeys as babies and birds as chickens. The word *mum*, Major concluded, served as the name for any four-legged animal for which the little boy lacked a name (Major, 1906).

Overextending the use of a word as a result of the application of inappropriate categorial criteria is a phenomenon commonly found in children at the age of around two. The word *ball*, for example, may be applied not only to balls but also to apples, oranges and door knobs, which all share the properties of being round and small. In fact, the shape of an object appears to be a common criterion for a child's first hypothesis about word meaning. Bowerman (1980) reports the case of Eva, who would use the word *moon* not only to refer to the real moon but also to a number of other crescent-shaped objects, such as grapefruit halves, lemon slices, curved cow-horns, a magnetic letter D etc. (cf. Aitchison, this volume). Overextensions such as these, where only one or two features of a word are picked out as criteria for the use of a particular word, have been widely documented and appear to be the same for children learning a variety of languages. In addition to shape, a number of other properties may be selected such as sound, smell or texture, as in the case of the small child who would use *bow-wow* for dogs, cats, scarves and fluffy bedroom slippers (Clark & Clark, 1977: 490).

There are also numerous studies of the difficulties experienced by small children trying to adjust their prototypes to adult ones, not only in the case of nouns but also in the case of words belonging to other word classes, such as verbs. When discussing closely-related members of the same category, it is often useful to view them as belonging to the same semantic field. One such semantic field of early importance to the young child is the field containing the verbs of possession. Here we find that a pair such as *give* and *take* is semantically simpler than a number of others. In the case of both verbs a form of transfer is involved. When transfer is initiated by the person with the object we use *give*, whereas *take* must be used if the person without the object initiates the transfer. Unfortunately, as soon as other factors enter the picture the situation ceases to be as straightforward. As soon as money is involved, an additional level of complexity is added and the exact meaning of words such as *buy*, *sell* and *trade* take considerably longer for children to sort out correctly. On the whole, the greater the complexity of a word, the later it is acquired. While *give* and *take* are understood early, studies of children between 3;6 and 8;6 who were asked to *give*, *buy* or *trade* objects in accordance with instructions, show that *buy*, *spend* and *sell* are yet to be mastered by most eight-year-olds (Clark & Clark, 1977: 485–514).

It is also not uncommon for children who have used a word correctly up to a certain age to suddenly start treating words, even those belonging to different semantic fields, as if they had the same meaning. Bowerman (1978) reports that having used *give* correctly when she was two, a year later Christie started to use *give* and *put* interchangeably: *Whenever Eva doesn't need the money, she gives (puts) it on my table*. It was to take an additional two years before Christie's use of *give* and *put* was correct by adult standards.

Another category of verb of immediate use to the child is the semantic field made up of the verbs of motion. In the most basic sense of something moving from one point to another, this category of verbs appears to be found in all languages (Viberg, 1988: 228). Motion also seems to be a feature of the world that children are able to register at a very early age. Bloom (1973) reports that at the age of nine months her daughter Alison used the word *car* only for cars moving in the street as she watched from her window. For Alison, it seemed, two conditions needed to be met for a four-wheeled vehicle to be categorised as a car: she had to see it and it had to be in motion. Cars standing still, cars in which she rode herself and cars in pictures did not qualify as 'cars'.

In the case of Alison, the concept of motion thus appears to have been a distinguishable feature at an early stage. This also seems to have been one of the characteristics selected by Eva as forming part of the meaning of the verb *kick* (Bowerman, 1978). At the age of 17 months Eva started to use *kick* to describe herself kicking a stationary object; then while looking at a picture of a cat with a ball of wool near its paw; then for a fluttering moth; then for cartoon turtles on television throwing their legs up; then when she threw something; then as she bumped a ball with the wheel of her tricycle, making it move. Using *kick* to refer to this wide range of activities seems to indicate that with experience Eva grew increasingly aware that the meaning of the verb *kick* could entail more than just impacting her foot into an object. It might also involve motion (the fluttering moth), a waving limb (the cartoon turtles), sudden contact with an object (the tricycle wheel) and an object being propelled (the ball). In the end she decided on someone kicking a ball as the prototype for the verb *kick*, which she appears to have analysed as possessing three main characteristics: a waving limb, sudden sharp contact between part of a body and an object, and propulsion forward of the object (Aitchison, 1994: 175).

These characteristics, selected by Eva on the basis of her observations of how the verb *kick* is used, may not be the same for other children, or for someone approaching English as an L2 learner. A typical feature of *kick* which is shared by a number of other verbs in English is that it is a lexicalisation doublet, which means that it may be used with or without an incorporated idea of motion. In *I kicked the wall with my left foot* the object being kicked remains stationary, but this is not the case in *I kicked the ball across the field with my left foot*. The basic sense of *kick* is, however, as it is used in the former case, where no movement of the kicked object is entailed (Talmy, 1985: 65).

Another example of such a lexicalisation doublet in English, a single verb form which, as we have seen, can be used either with or without an incorporated idea of motion, is the verb *float*. In its basic usage, *float* refers to the buoyancy relation between an object and a medium, as in *The craft floated/was afloat on a cushion of air*. But the same verb also has a second usage which combines the idea of buoyancy with that of motion, as in *The craft floated into the hangar on a cushion of air* (Talmy, 1985: 64). This shows that in one of its uses *float*, just like *kick*, can express two concepts at once — motion and its manner. Languages which allow the conflation of motion and manner in this way usually have a whole series of verbs in common use that express motion occurring in various manners. English is a good example of this type of language, as are all branches of Indo-European languages except (post-Latin) Romance (Talmy, 1985: 62). In the Romance languages, manner must instead be expressed in a different way, for example through a separate constituent:

La botella entró a la cueva flotando
the bottle moved-into the cave floating
'The bottle floated into the cave.'

Thus children growing up speaking a Romance language as their L1 will learn to express manner through other lexical and syntactic means, separate from the motion verb. But as a variety of verbs express manner in combination with motion in all other Indo-European languages, a reanalysis of the prototypical characteristics of the motion verbs would need to form part of the learning process for a Romance L1 speaker wishing to learn a non-Romance language. On the other hand, for L1 speakers of other Indo-European languages it has to be borne in mind that motion and manner may not be lexicalised in the same way in the Romance languages. This is easier said than done, however, to judge from the frequency with which students of French forget that sentences such as *He ran down the hill* need to be converted into *He descended the hill, while running* for appropriate rendering into French.

Second Language Acquisition

Recent research on prototype development seems to point to the overall conclusion that L1 learners take a long time to become aware of adult native speakers' treatment of categories, and that even fluent non-native speakers may never be fully in possession of this knowledge (Aitchison, 1992: 78). One obvious way of trying, pedagogically, to overcome this problem would be to compare and contrast different lexical categories in the SL and the TL. However, the wisdom of applying a contrastive analysis to SL and TL has been hotly debated. During the 1970s criticism of contrastive analysis was particularly strong, focusing on its claim that it could make predictions about language learning, based on observed differences between SL and TL (Wardhaugh, 1974). However, given what we now know about linguistic typology and universals, an analysis of contrasting features in SL and TL based on cross-linguistic studies of typological features may prove more fruitful in producing testable predictions than the often purely structural comparisons of traditional contrastive analysis. It would, for instance, help us to show where, in a particular language, marked *vis-à-vis* unmarked constructions may be found. In linguistics, markedness is 'a term used to describe a kind of prototype effect — a form of asymmetry in a category where one member or subcategory is taken to be somehow more basic than the other (or others)' (Lakoff, 1987: 60–1). It is above all with respect to this asymmetry or prototype effect that some interesting observations have been made with respect to L2 acquisition, in particular in relation to the acquisition of verbs.

The existence of four well-developed, open word classes appears to be a characteristic feature of European languages in general: nouns, verbs, adjectives and adverbs (Viberg, 1990a: 391). Although each of these classes has several thousand members, some words seem to be used much more frequently than others. The tendency to favour a limited set of words appears to be most pronounced in the case of verbs (Viberg, 1990a: 397). With respect to their basic meaning, these core or 'nuclear' verbs[1] (Viberg, 1990a,b) show a number of similarities among the European languages, forming a semantic nucleus inside the category to which they belong. Such categories include verbs of motion (*go*), production (*do*), possession (*give, take*), perception (*see*), cognition (*know*) and verbal communication (*say*).

In terms of frequency of use, these nuclear verbs rank high in all European languages (Viberg, 1990b: 27). The majority of them are also the most frequently found verbs in some non-European languages, such as Arabic and Chinese. These two properties of nuclear verbs, that is, a high frequency in individual languages and a wide typological distribution, are also characteristic features of unmarked lexical elements. In addition, such elements also tend to have a number of secondary meanings, function as syntactic prototypes and be favoured at an early stage by L1 as well as L2 learners (Viberg, 1990a: 397–9).

Since they are acquired early and occur with great frequency, the use of nuclear verbs becomes a conditioned response at an early stage in both L1 and L2 learners. But while all language learners are likely to rely on certain frequently-occurring lexical items until they have acquired a larger vocabulary, L2 speakers tend to do so to an even greater extent than L1 learners. As other parts of their grammar demand greater overall attention, the processing capacity of L2 learners is also under greater strain. As a result, a tendency may develop to rely heavily on a small set of well-known lexical items, leading to pronounced overuse of nuclear verbs in the language of L2 speakers.

A number of studies on the use of nuclear verbs among L2 speakers point to such overuse. Migrant L2 learners of Swedish who were asked to describe a set of pictures showed a clear tendency to let the verb *gå* (go, walk) represent any verb of motion for which they had not yet acquired the appropriate word. Trying to describe a series of pictures in Swedish showing a child involved in an accident and being thrown out of a car window, speakers of languages as far apart linguistically as Spanish and Finnish would describe what happened to the child as *och här barnet [...] gå ut igenom fönster* (and here the child [...] go out through window) (Viberg, 1988: 227). Independent of their L1, learners seem to pick out one or two nuclear verbs inside each semantic field for use in place of verbs they do not as yet know. In the Swedish study, the two verbs of motion used repeatedly were *gå* (go) and *komma* (come) (Viberg, 1988: 227). It is interesting to note, however, that these two verbs appear to be favoured at different stages in the L2 acquisition process. As shown by Kotsinas' study of migrant Greek L2 learners of Swedish, *komma* first seems to function as the overall verb of motion. Later, and at a more advanced stage, *gå* tends to replace *komma* (Kotsinas, 1985: 35). This also appears to be the tendency observed in the case of L2 learners of German. The Heidelberg project discussed by Viberg (1985: 31–3), a study of migrant L2 learners of German with a Romance language background, also shows early overextended use of *kommen*, as shown below (the interlanguage German version is shown to the left with the target version in parenthesis):

Ich nicht komme nach Espana   (Ich konnte nicht nach Spanien fahren)
I not come to Spain   *I could not to Spain go*
'I could not go to Spain'

Alfred komme Bier (Alfred bringt Bier)
'Alfred brings beer'

The verb *kommen* also seems to replace verbs drawn from other, quite different semantic fields, such as, for instance, *anfangen* (begin), *bekommen* (get) and *werden* (become). At higher levels of proficiency, however, the frequency of *kommen* decreases markedly. The Heidelberg project findings are also confirmed by studies of Swedish L1 speakers learning French, which show early overextended use of *venir* (come) (Viberg, 1985: 37–8). In this study, Karl, one of the subjects tested, initially tended to use *vient* consistently as an overall verb of motion. Two months later, however, he had moved on to using *aller* (go) in this capacity, while the use of *venir* was no longer overextended, paralleling the stages of development in L2 learners' acquisition of German.

It seems, then, that from the knowledge L2 learners have of their own language, they have some kind of intuition that verbs belonging to a particular semantic field have a common nucleus. As a result, they seem to be 'on the look-out' for nuclear verbs in the TL. Finding a nuclear verb in the new language then makes it possible for them to make themselves understood while moving inside the whole of the semantic field to which this verb belongs, making strategic use of the lexical base structure that all languages seem to share.

Translation

Early reliance on a limited set of lexical elements among migrant L2 learners is also likely to be reinforced by the register of language to which they are most frequently exposed. With L2 normally learnt at the workplace, initial encounter with the TL is likely to be in its spoken form, often colloquial and informal, with basic core words and non-specific references figuring prominently. As these linguistic features appear to be characteristic of the language of everyday situations, it would seem reasonable to expect them to occur with relatively high frequency in popular fiction and, as a result, in translations of texts written in this genre. This, however, does not always seem to happen.

In a comparative study of vocabulary used in Swedish novels, and in novels translated from English into Swedish, Gellerstam (1985) discusses some characteristics of so-called 'translationese'. One feature of this phenomenon, it emerges, is the overuse of certain words in translated texts which normally occur with low frequency in texts originally written in the SL. As an illustration, Gellerstam discusses the case of the English verb *arrive*, consistently rendered as *anlända* in translation into Swedish.

However, unlike *arrive* in English, the use of the verb *anlända* in Swedish is restricted to certain registers of formal style, in particular official timetables referring to arrivals of trains and planes at specified times. A typical example of a verb expected to be used with low frequency in most Swedish texts, *anlända* nevertheless occurs with relatively high frequency in translation.

We recall that nuclear verbs tend to be associated with the characteristics of unmarked lexical items. They are acquired early by both L1 and L2 learners; they often function as syntactic prototypes; and they seem to have a number of secondary meanings. In Swedish it is common for nuclear verbs to acquire a different or slightly altered meaning through the addition of a particle. In this way *komma* (come) may combine with a number of different particles, one of which is *fram* (along, forward) yielding *komma fram* (arrive) which in its frequency of use corresponds closely to the use of *arrive* in English. This fact, however, is not reflected in the translated texts. The lesson here for translators, it would seem, is the need for closer attention to the importance of frequency of occurrence (cf. Koller, 1992). If this dimension is overlooked, what may happen is that a marked form in the TL might inadvertently take the place of an unmarked form in the SL. Or, viewed in terms of categorisation, by opting for a verb from a subordinate rather than a basic level, translators unwittingly add an element of 'translationese' to the target text (TT).

Why then do these translated texts so uniformly show the use of a low-frequency word, a word which translators themselves are not likely to use to any great extent in spontaneous spoken or written language? Gellerstam provides us with a possible answer to this question when he points out that any Swedish speaker, asked for the equivalent to the verb *arrive*, will unhesitatingly answer *anlända*. In other words, *anlända* appears to be a verb which is readily used in translation but rarely in spontaneous speech. Why should this be the case?

The answer may perhaps be traced back to learning practices at school, to the learning of lexical items in vocabulary lists in textbooks with undifferentiated equivalents, or to learners' dictionaries containing inadequate semantic information (cf. Rogers, this volume). Ironically, the inappropriate lexical equivalent may have stuck, not as the result of insufficient linguistic competence but simply because the word was learnt so early on. Part and parcel of the ease of early acquisition may be the lack of awareness that more than a single dimension is involved in establishing the equivalence of lexical items between the SL and the TL. This in turn points to the importance of pedagogical strategies when teaching L2 vocabulary, whether these involve translation or reference to other semantically-related L2 words, such as synonyms, antonyms or hyponyms. Gellerstam's observations would certainly seem to lend some support to the latter approach.

Yet another feature of 'translationese' is the stylistic awkwardness that may result when the process of translation requires expansion in the TT of certain items in the source text (ST). As Nida & Taber (1969) point out, a good translation often tends to be longer than the original, because the transfer of a text from one linguistic and cultural structure to another may require expansion if all information contained in the SL is to be maintained in the TL. The problem this poses for the translator is to decide precisely how much of the original needs to be retained and how much can be left implicit for the reader.

We recall that in the previous discussion of L1 acquisition it was noted that Romance L1 speakers are likely to need to adjust their motion verb prototypes when learning another Indo-European language. So while the Indo-European languages, and in addition Chinese, belong to a typological group of languages in which the verb can express at once motion *and* manner, Spanish and other Romance languages constitute exceptions, belonging to a different group. As a result, in a translation from English into Spanish involving the verb *float* (see above), the translator would need to make a decision as to whether manner needs to be expressed explicitly through a separate constituent (Talmy, 1985: 69):

The balloon floated up the chimney:
El globo subió por la chimenea (flotando)
the balloon moved-up through the chimney (floating)

The Spanish verb in this sentence expresses path as well as motion. Manner, however, can only be expressed as an independent, usually adverbial or gerundive type constituent. This means that, in a translation into Spanish of *The balloon floated up the chimney*, we are inevitably going to end up with a longer and perhaps stylistically somewhat awkward TT, if all features of the ST are to be retained.

The question then arises whether all features of the ST really need to be expressed as explicitly in the TT. The answer to this question is best provided by the translator who, with time and experience, will learn how information explicit in the ST may be redistributed, lexically and syntactically, in the TT, or even omitted altogether. Just as children will learn to recognise the relevant distinctions in their L1, so translators will grow sensitive to which features can and need to be expressed explicitly in the TT. Or, to put it in cross-linguistic terms, they will know that while in principle it is possible to perceive any number of distinctions in the organisation of the world around us, only some of them are manifested linguistically because the grammar of a particular language 'may provide no rules for tying them to surface structures of sentences' (Schlesinger, 1982: 70).

As young children learn to interpret their environment, they also start to create an internal model of the world. This organisation of experience has been referred to as 'framing': '...we must add to the description of grammar and lexicon a description of the cognitive and interactional "frames" in terms of which the language user interprets his environment...' (Fillmore, 1976: 23). It is possible to distinguish a number of different frames such as, for instance, the social event frame of greetings, structured in accordance with the customs and practice of the language of the country in which they take place. Another such frame is the commercial event frame, containing verbs such as *cost, spend, charge, profit, bargain,* and so on. The meaning of many of these verbs, which involve the exchange of goods and services against money, are, as we have seen already, sufficiently complex to baffle young children for some time. And having passed the first hurdle of trying to sort out what all these terms mean in our own language, we might later, as L2, L3 etc. learners, need to go through the same process yet again, relearning aspects of the organisation of buying and selling, as this may take different forms in different cultures and languages.

Matching cultural frames is also an important and sometimes difficult task for the translator. Even between the relatively isomorphic German and American commercial event frames, for instance, there are a number of differences, including transactions such as American mortgage and instalment loans, which are unfamiliar concepts in Germany. And as soon as we venture further afield, differences become increasingly more striking. In an Arabic-speaking commercial situation, price does not necessarily involve a fixed amount but is open to bargaining and negotiation in a way which is alien to large parts of Europe (Neubert & Shreve, 1993: 61).

It is in the context of matching cultural frames with the aim of pinpointing differences between SL and TL that Neubert and Shreve point to the usefulness of prototype theory for translators. They see it as the practising translator's main task to apply a form of prototype analysis to examples of texts concerned with the relevant cultural frame event. The texts chosen for such an analysis are background texts, all representative samples of discourse that readers and listeners of the TL are used to expecting under identical or similar communicative conditions. This means in practice, to take one of Neubert's examples, that a translator engaged to translate the British Highway Code into French would be well advised to study *La Code de la Route*, while a translator working into German would benefit from familiarising him or herself with *Die Straßenverkehrsordnung* (Neubert, 1981: 135). The textual profiles resulting from such analyses would then serve as a guide to the translator in identifying the appropriate TL features. This in turn would make it possible for the translator to 'retexture' the SL text into the TL text, monitoring its development by guiding the process of conformity to the prototype.

The notion of prototypes in the context of translation is also used by Snell-Hornby (1993). Discussing translation between German and English, Snell-Hornby distinguishes between five basic groups of prototypes (1993: 108-9), reproduced here in abridged form:

(1) Terminology/nomenclature
    English: *Oxygen*; German: *Sauerstoff*
(2) Internationally-known items and sets
    English: *Saturday*; German: *Sonnabend*
(3) Concrete objects, basic level items
    English: *chair*; German: *Stuhl*
(4) Words expressing perception and evaluation, often linked to sociocultural norms
    English: *bleak*; German: ?
    German: *gemütlich*; English: ?
(5) Culture-bound elements
    English: *wicket*; German: ?
    German: *Pumpernickel*; English: ?

Snell-Hornby points out that in (1)–(5) the concept of equivalence becomes increasingly more difficult to apply. It can easily be applied to prototypes (1) and (2), correlating with sharply-defined technical terms as well as with items whose referent is, if not universally valid, at least common to the two language communities concerned. Prototypes (4) and (5), on the other hand, represent items below the basic level exemplified in prototype (3). In these cases the concept of equivalence is less applicable, resulting in an increase in translation difficulties.

Culture-bound elements of the kind exemplified in (5) usually constitute unknown concepts in the TL, and in the case of such gaps or lacunae borrowing is often the simplest translation procedure, for example, the way English has acquired *tortilla* from Spanish and *sauna* from Finnish (Vinay & Darbelnet, 1969). This leaves us with the words in (4) which, as Snell-Hornby puts it, 'express perception and evaluation, often linked to sociocultural norms'. Words such as these will always remain a problem in translation and a successful solution is usually dependent on the skill and sensitivity of the individual translator. However, returning now to Aitchison's introductory discussion of prototype theory, we can recall that recent developments have focused on an offshoot of this theory, which is concerned with covert mental models. One way of revealing such idealised models, it has been suggested, might be through everyday metaphors (Lakoff & Johnson, 1980). Looking more closely at these metaphors, we may find, for instance, that while some of the mental models they contain seem to be universal and apply across cultures, others appear to be culture specific. As is well known, metaphors constitute a minefield for the translator if they are to be transferred intact from SL to TL (cf. for instance, Kloepfer, 1967; Dagut, 1976; Newmark, 1982). In conclusion, then, it may be noted that this appears to be yet another area where translation theory might again be able to draw on the findings of linguistics. And, given the impetus for discussion and research that the notion of prototypes has already provided, there would seem to be little doubt that further enquiry into this area may similarly yield linguistic findings of potential interest to the translator.

Conclusion

This paper has considered the insights yielded by so-called prototype theory with respect to L1 and L2 acquisition as well as to the field of translation studies. In addition to the observations that have already been made by a number of linguists in these three fields, it has been shown that translation studies, still a young discipline, may benefit from the insights already gained in the field of L1 and L2 acquisition. The notion of the prototype, however, is only one of the concepts that may be of shared interest to translator and linguist. As new and interesting issues in linguistics come to the fore, new areas of potential benefit to the translator are also likely to emerge.

Notes

1. Where foreign language sources have been quoted, all translations are my own.

References

AITCHISON, J. 1992, Good birds, better birds and amazing birds: the development of prototypes. In P.J.L. ARNAUD and H. BEJOINT (eds) *Vocabulary and Applied Linguistics* (pp. 71–84). London: Macmillan.
— 1994, *Words in the Mind. An Introduction to the Mental Lexicon* 2nd edn. Oxford: Blackwell.

BERLIN, B. 1978, Ethnobiological classification. In E. ROSCH and B. LLOYD (eds) *Cognition and Categorisation* (pp. 9–26). Hillsdale, NJ: Lawrence Erlbaum Associates.
BLOOM, L.M. 1973, *One Word at a Time: The Use of Single Word Utterances Before Syntax*. The Hague: Mouton.
BOWERMAN, M. 1978, Systematising semantic knowledge: Changes over time in the child's organisation of meaning. *Child Development* 49, 977–87.
— 1980, The structure and origin of semantic categories in the language learning child. In D. FOSTER and S. BRANDES (eds) *Symbol as Sense: New Approaches to the Analysis of Meaning* (pp. 277–99). New York: Academic Press.
CLARK, H.H. and CLARK, E.V. 1977, *Psychology and Language. An Introduction to Psycholinguistics*. New York: Harcourt Brace Jovanovich.
DAGUT, M.B. 1976, Can metaphor be translated? *Babel* xxxiii (1), 21–33.
FILLMORE, C.J. 1976, Frame semantics and the nature of language. *Annals of the New York Academy of Science* 280, 20–31.
GELLERSTAM, M. 1985, Translationese in Swedish novels translated from English. In L. WOLLIN, and H. LINDQUIST (eds) *Translation Studies in Scandinavia*. Proceedings from the Scandinavian Symposium on Translation Theory. SSOTT II, 88–95, Lund 14–15 June 1985. Lund: CWK Gleerup.
KLOEPFER, R. 1967, *Die Theorie der literarischen Übersetzung*. Munich: Wilhelm Fink Verlag.
KOLLER, W. 1992, *Einführung in die Übersetzungswissenschaft* 4th edn. Heidelberg: Quelle & Meyer.
KOTSINAS, U-B. 1985, *Invandrare talar svenska*. Ord och stil. Malmö: Liber.
LAKOFF, G. 1987, *Women, Fire and Dangerous Things. What Categories Reveal About the Mind*. Chicago: University of Chicago Press.
LAKOFF, G and JOHNSON, M. 1980, *Metaphors We Live By*. Chicago: University of Chicago Press.
MAJOR, D.R. 1906, *First Steps in Mental Growth*. New York: Macmillan.
NEUBERT, A. 1981, Translation, interpreting and text linguistics. In B. SIGURD and J. SVARTVIK (eds) AILA 81 Proceedings: Lectures. *Studia Linguistica* 35, 130–45.
NEUBERT, A. and SHREVE, G.M. 1993, *Translation as Text*. Kent, Ohio: Kent State University Press.
NEWMARK, P. 1982, *Approaches to Translation*. Oxford: Pergamon Press.
NIDA, E.A. and TABER C.R. 1969, *The Theory and Practice of Translation. Help for Translators* Vol. 8. Prepared under the auspices of the United Bible Societies. Leiden: E.J. Brill.
ROSCH, E. 1973, Natural categories. *Cognitive Psychology* 4, 328–50.
— 1975, Cognitive representations of semantic categories. *Journal of Experimental Psychology: General* 104, 192–233.
ROSCH, E. and LLOYD, B.B. (eds) 1978, *Cognition and Categorisation*. Hillsdale, NJ: Lawrence Erlbaum.
SCHLESINGER, I.M. 1982, *Steps to Language: Toward a Theory of Native Language Acquisition*. Hillsdale, NJ: Lawrence Erlbaum Associates.
SNELL-HORNBY, M. 1993, Word against text: The role of semantics in translation. In G. JÄGER and K. GOMMLICH (eds) *Text and Meaning* (pp. 105–12). Kent, Ohio: Kent State University Press.

THE WORD IS MY OYSTER 55

TALMY, L. 1985, Lexicalisation patterns: Semantic structure in lexical forms. In T. SHOPEN (ed.) *Language Typology and Syntactic Description*. Vol III: *Grammatical Categories and the Lexicon*. Cambridge: Cambridge University Press.

VIBERG, Å. 1985, Lexikal andraspråksinlärning. Hur polsk-, spansk — och finsk — språkiga lär in svenskans placeraverb. In M. AXELSSON and Å VIBERG (eds) *SUM — rapport 2* (pp.5–92).

— 1988, Ordförråd och ordinlärning. Några utgångspunkter för en studie av hur ordförrådet lärs in. In K.HYLTENSTAM and I. LINDBERG (eds) *Första Symposiet om Svenska som Andra Språk* (pp. 215–33). Centrum för tvåspråkighetsforskning, Stockholm University.

— 1990a, Svenskans lexikala profil. In E. ANDERSSON and M. SUNDMAN (eds) *Svenskans Beskrivning 17* (pp. 391–408). Åbo: Åbo Academy Press.

— 1990b, Språkinlärning och språkundervisning. In V. ADELSWÄRD and N.F. DAVIES (eds) *På väg mot ett nytt språk* (pp. 1–40). Rapport från ASLA: s höstsymposium. Linköping, 9–10 November 1990.

VINAY, J.P. and DARBELNET J. 1969, *Stylistique Comparée du Français et de l'Anglais* 2nd edn. Paris: Didier.

WARDHAUGH, R. 1974, The contrastive analysis hypothesis. In J. SCHUMANN and N. STENSON (eds) *New Frontiers in Second Language Learning* (pp. 11–19). Rowley, MA: Newbury House.

5 Looking at English Words in Translation

PETER NEWMARK

Five years ago I wrote a paper called 'Words and Text: Words and their Degree of Context in Translation', subsequently published in *About Translation* (Newmark, 1991). I now propose to reconsider its conclusion:

> 'Contrary to the prevailing wisdom, many single source language (SL) words in texts (e.g. 'haematology' or even 'houses') often have perfect translation equivalence, referentially and pragmatically, with their target language (TL) correspondents, whatever their degree of context, but the perfect translation of a text — and therefore the principle of perfect equivalence for texts — does not exist.'

I think this statement is broadly true, but it needs to be qualified.

Typically, only certain technical terms such as German *Gefluder*, French *flume*, English *flume* (artificial channel for a stream of water to be applied to some industrial use) and international institutional terms (e.g. UNESCO) have perfect translation equivalence on all occasions; the remaining words only have perfect translation equivalence in respect of the message to be conveyed, not of the nuances of meaning in the word. Thus *Grüße ihn von mir* for *Send him my love* conveys the essential message, but the meaning conveyed is only approximate; furthermore, *That's a large house* for *Das ist ein großes Haus* is not a perfect equivalent, as the first sentence may imply a different criterion for size, and assume a different cultural image of a house. It is also possible that the German *Haus* is a wider and more common word than the English *house*, overlapping with words such as *building*, *premises* and *home* in the associative field.

Owing to the intensive work of the International Organisation for Standardisation (ISO), as well as a number of national standards organisations, the number of terms with exact translation equivalence in the languages of the industrially-developed countries has greatly increased. Various technologies in countries with Romance, Germanic, Slavonic and other languages have drawn from a common stock of Greek and Latin words, and have created an infrastructure of technical, scientific and academic terms which serve as a unifying and intertranslatable resource for the languages of the developed countries, and are likely to serve an increasing number of developing countries. (Misguided or not, this is one of the reasons why the SWAPO government has decided to make English the only official language in Namibia; further, if an African language such as Herero had been preferred, it would have sharpened interethnic rivalries.) To this extent, an exponentially-increasing number of SL terms are likely to have near perfect translation equivalence with their TL correspondents, bearing in mind that there will always be extraordinary linguistic gaps and false friends even in technical areas.

If we consider the four open word classes — nouns, verbs, adjectives and adverbs — we find that nouns representing common objects are most likely to have perfect translation equivalents in another language, leaving aside cultural variations, provided the objects have the same functions and approximate shapes and colours, and are not used figuratively. Thus: *window, Fenster, fenêtre, finestra* in English, German, French and Italian, respectively. Since verbs often combine movement or displacement with the manner of doing so in different ways in different languages, as Anderman's contribution also indicates, they are less likely than nouns to find perfect equivalents; adjectives or adverbs represent human qualities which are often culturally modified by value judgements — e.g. *patient* and *patiently* from *patience* — and have the least accurate correspondences.

Further, in the basic word stock, where the English language's triple principal antecedents (Germanic, French and Grecolatin) are apparent, we may acknowledge a tripartite division of register, as in the case of *begin, commence* and *initiate*. When we consider non-technical language, it becomes increasingly clear that amongst the languages of the developed countries, English has a special place as regards translation equivalence: when it names human and natural qualities, it can be both wider and more approximate (e.g. *nice, nasty* for which it appears foreign language equivalents are hard to find) and more particular and detailed (e.g. *fussy, finicky*). In principle, objects are likely to be more closely apprehended, but in fact this is not so, since below a certain level of generality they are likely to become cultural (e.g. *Moulton* or *Brompton* for *bike*...) (cf. Anderman, this volume).

The cardinal fact is that English, in many estimates, has more than three times as many words as any other language (cf. for example, Claiborne, 1990); therefore, linguistically, its 'world picture' is likely to be more detailed and particular. Large English dictionaries have 400,000–600,000 words (the *OED* has 615,000; *Webster* has 450,000) — compared to other language dictionaries, such as Russian with 150,000 and French with 130,000 — my guess is that German has 250,000–300,000. Compare this with Bryson's (1990) figures: 200,000 words are in common English use compared with 184,000 in German and 100,000 in French.

The fanning out of English into worldwide national varieties also weighs against finding translation equivalences in other languages. Further, in the area of cultural focus, where other languages have their *snow*, *camels*, *cheeses*, *sausages*, *wines* etc., English has its notorious abundance of predominant standard cricket images (cricket ousts music when test matches are broadcast on Radio 3). Since these normally either have to be reduced to sense or be transferred to another image in translation, the translation loss is considerable (e.g. *be on a sticky wicket*: *in der Klemme sein* in German). Any retention of the cricket imagery would be incomprehensible in translation. Due to its worldwide contacts with other languages, I assume that English has the largest common or standard figurative and idiomatic linguistic stock, again making translation more difficult.

Bryson (1990) is in fact mistaken when he states that English has nothing 'to match *sang-froid*, *glasnost* or *macho*', since these are now three common English words and they could arguably be satisfactorily replaced by their hyperonyms *cool*, *transparency* and *sexist*. It is indeed difficult to say when a word is adopted — or, in German, 'eingebürgert' — into another language. *Collins English Dictionary* puts *crème*, *crème caramel*, *crème de cacao*, *crème de menthe* and *crème fraiche* in roman type, but *crème brûlée* and *crème de la crème* are put in italics and marked as French; yet *crème de la crème* is I think more commonly used in English than *crème fraiche* or *crème de cacao*. Note, however, that these instances in particular may in time come to illustrate English lexical increase, since their referents are likely to be prepared according to new English recipes.

Whilst it is (rather too) obvious that one typically translates texts and not languages, any act of translation has contrastive linguistics as one of its frames of reference. Translation theory (in its wider sense, encompassing the translation procedures and options at any rank in a text) is enriched by contrastive linguistics, which is a dynamic discipline continuously having to deal with changing language and changing use of language, the latter noticeably affecting slang, idioms, technical terms and single spoken words considerably earlier than it modifies grammar. Nevertheless, I would suggest that not only English lexis, but also English grammar, is constantly being enriched since it has been and is still being subjected to varied linguistic and cultural influences and impacts. Such an idea would surprise the many who still mistakenly think that English, having shed most of its inflections (few conjugations or declensions to learn), 'has little grammar'.

In fact, English appears to be unique among European languages in having three present tenses, two of which (the progressive and the emphatic) sometimes translate rather clumsily into the languages that lack them. English also has a verb plus -*ing* form, rare in the multiplicity of its functions and in its complexity. No two grammars appear to agree on the appropriate terms for these forms: gerund, verb noun, verbal noun, participial clause, participial adjective, present participle, deverbal adjective, deverbal noun. Moreover, often one or other of its uses is omitted. I shall illustrate this verb plus -*ing* form with the examples in (1)–(11). In the first two examples the verb -*ing* construction represents respectively a state and a process. Other contrasts include that between (9) and (10), where the -*ing* form of the verb *sing* in (10), *singing*, represents a process, whereas the construction in (9), *rendering*, does not:

(1) The charming fool.
(2) The winking fool.
(3) I like singing/to sing.
(4) Singing pleases me.
(5) I am surprised at him singing.
(6) I am surprised at his singing.
(7) Singing a song is agreeable.
(8) His singing the song pleases me.
(9) His rendering of the song was good.
(10) His singing of the song was good.
(11) The singing pleases me.

In my opinion, the -*ing* form (or 'gerund': *founding the school*), is more informal and more frequently used than the deverbal noun (*the foundation of the school*) or an infinitive (*to found the school*). For this reason, it is often useful, when translating, to make standard transpositions as shown in examples (12a) and (12b), and (13a) and (13b). In translating (12a), the deverbal noun in (12c), *the privatisation of a public utility*, should be reserved for more formal registers. In (13), the infinitive in (13c), *opportunity to do it*, should be reserved for situations where the main verb is in the future in French.

(12) (a) La privatisation d'un service public.
    (b) Privatising a public utility.
    (c) The privatisation of a public utility.

(13) (a) Je n'avais pas d'occasion de le faire.
   (b) I had no opportunity of doing it.
   (c) I had no opportunity to do it.

In many contexts, the -*ing* construction, originally a verb here functioning syntactically as a noun, is more versatile than its equivalents, which are typically exemplified by infinitives, verbal nouns or relative clauses.

English grammar also allows the conversion of word classes, thus enriching the vocabulary even further. For instance, a usually monosyllabic verb may be converted into a noun (occasionally, a noun into a verb, e.g. *stone, fire,*) or a present participle into a noun, e.g. *parting*. *Round* may in fact belong to any one of the four open word classes, as well as being a preposition.

English also has a large number of modal-type verbs: *shall, will, should, would, may, might, can, could, must, have to, is to, due to, wish to, want to, dare, need to, need, used to*. Here again, English can embrace the meaning of another language more closely, since its variety of modals makes it more selective and gives it greater force. In contrast, the range of English modal particles that rather colloquially convey propositions to receptors appears to be smaller than that of some other languages (e.g. Italian, *magari, ecco*; German, *ja, nun*; or French, *voilà*), so that here translation into English often loses force.

The English prepositional system also differs from, for instance, the Romance languages, having less need to resort to verbal constructions (cf. *situé sur, on*) or prepositional phrases (cf. *au niveau de, at*). There is also an interesting set of 'link' or 'equative' verbs: *go, grow, become, turn, wax* (obsolescent), *get, turn out, turn to, change to, come to be*, all followed by an adjective, which can sometimes be accounted for, but less expressively, in other languages by reflexive verbs or adverbs.

Paradoxically, in spite of losing most of its inflexions, English has a more abundant derivational morphology than other languages in terms of its many prefixes and suffixes inherited from its linguistic antecedents, but in comparison with other European languages, particularly Italian, it is less abundant in suffixes of dimension and depreciation (*-accio, -issimo* etc.), and so has less 'diminishing' force at the lexical level in these areas.

The main area of 'lexicogrammar' (the large area between grammar and lexis — the term was created and then apparently abandoned by Halliday) in English is the huge family of so-called phrasal constructions, i.e. verbs, nouns, adjectives (past participles that have become stative, e.g. *run down, worn out*) and particles (*he's down, it's off*), which flooded into the language at the beginning of the century, being progressively less frowned on as

Latin released its prescriptive hold amongst the style-setters. Mainly, these constructions consist of monosyllabic verbs (rather more Germanic than Romance) with particles, frequently with more than one meaning; their informality, unpretentiousness and vividness often cannot be adequately translated into another language — they are, I think, the largest linguistic rather than cultural obstacle in many translations from English.

Phrasal verbs have either one or two particles with adverbial or prepositional functions; they may be transitive and/or intransitive (*He blew up the gasworks/The gasworks blew up*); they continue to multiply and, on the whole, tend to originate as colloquialisms (*chip in*), but may be neutral in tone (*move out, come in*). They are normally characterised by their simplicity, vividness, force and neatness. It is always possible to translate them fully as 'message', but in respect of 'meaning' their translation 'yield' will depend on their denotative quality, which is high in *He came in* but not in *He popped in*, and their neatness in the TL (cf. Newmark, 1982). In the majority of cases, it will only be possible to faintly hint at the succinct feel of a phrasal construction in a foreign language (*cop out*: *échappatoire* and *excuse facile* in French; and *Rückzieher* in German).

In principle, any intransitive phrasal verb (with one particle) can become a colloquial phrasal noun (*a sleep-in, a sit-in, a lie-down*). Phrasal verbs, transitive or intransitive, occasionally become stative adjectives (*run-down, built-in, built-up*). Again, it is normally the denotations rather than the connotations that are transferred in the translations, which are not as simple or vivid.

I am suggesting that for three reasons English is often less amenable to translation than other languages, while at the same time it also has the resources to encompass the meaning of other languages rather more comprehensively. First, it has enormous synonymic power and great grammatical range. Secondly, it has a set of phrasal constructions which cover colloquial and neutral, and particularly informal registers which are poorly served in many other languages; they can handily steer a text from a formal, e.g. (*descend*) to an informal (*go down*) to a slang (*flop down*) tone, and back again. And finally, we can add the fact that the language has never been lexically and grammatically controlled by a national academy; for this reason, it has admitted words from other parts of the world more freely than many other languages: it has been left free to 'embrace' other languages, more so than those which have a history of isolation or subjection to official rules and regulations.

Nevertheless, since all languages have to and can be translated more or less accurately, any assessment of their amenability to translation or their capacity for translating has to be treated cautiously. The great early nineteenth-century Italian poet Leopardi (Leopardi, 1816, in Gillespie, 1992) said that Italian, being an aggregate of languages, had the greatest capacity to adapt to foreign forms; French, which had become so remote in structure and pronunciation from its Latin origins, was now 'resistant and homogenised', and had less capacity to translate than any other language — he did not mention the influence of the French Academy; German was rich and various but lacked a character of its own, and German translations imitated words rather than things; it therefore missed expressing the genius and the force of the foreign language and of the original author (Leopardi, 1816). Such generalisations have a certain truth, but they are unfortunately lacking in examples. Moreover, Leopardi does not mention national cultures, which are the most important factor in assessing a language's amenability to translation.

In respect of 'message', translation between any languages can be perfect; in respect of 'meaning' there is always a deficit of some kind (cf. Newmark, 1982). I have tried to demonstrate that the particular characteristics of English are responsible for an imbalance in its communicative exchanges with other languages (since at present English is increasingly becoming the world language of communication), but that these usually only become apparent when language is stretched to express thought at its most subtle and most difficult. And finally, I must insist that these are only general, background, reference considerations pertaining to language; in a particular translation task, more immediate cultural factors become more important. Equally decisive are the personal skills and sensitivity of the translator, which can outweigh all the positive or negative arguments in this paper, which in many places are speculative as well as tentative.

References

BRYSON, B. 1990, *Mother Tongue: The English Language*. Harmondsworth: Penguin.
CLAIBORNE, R. 1990, *The Life and Times of the English Language*. London: Bloomsbury.
LEOPARDI, G. (1992), Leopardi on the right language of translation. In S. GILLESPIE (ed.) *Translation and Literature* Vol 1 (pp. 141–8). Edinburgh: Edinburgh University Press.
NEWMARK, P. 1982, *Approaches to Translation*. Oxford: Pergamon Press.
— 1991, *About Translation*. Clevedon: Multilingual Matters.

6 Lexical Innovation: Neologism and Dictionaries

JOHN AYTO

The great nineteenth-century dictionaries — epitomised by the *Oxford English Dictionary* — have bequeathed us the image of the dictionary as museum, more interested in the past than in current developments. Aspects of that legacy remain with us — the 1988 *Chambers English Dictionary*, for example, still gives 'an assembly, parliament' as the first meaning of *thing*, and defines *fetch* as 'a stratagem' — but present-day dictionaries increasingly resemble not so much museums as supermarkets. All the words entered have sell-by dates — if they become obsolescent they will very likely be removed from the next edition — and lexicographers are more and more on the lookout for new lines — neologisms.

Indeed, now more than ever dictionary publishers use the number of 'new words' in a dictionary as the key marketing point in its favour, regardless of whatever other merits it may have (the 1986 edition of the *Collins English Dictionary*, for instance, was hailed by its advertisers for its 'over 7,000 new headwords'). This promotion of the 'cabinet of novelties' image does as little to foster public understanding of the qualities of good dictionaries as did the old museum stereotype (cf. O'Kill, 1988).

A notable by-product of this increasing attention given to new words is the number of English dictionaries that have appeared over the last 20 years specifically devoted to neologisms, and in this chapter I wish to examine what light they cast on the processes of lexical innovation. First I need to distinguish two sorts of 'new-word' dictionary, compiled with very different aims and methods. First, there is the supplement to an existing dictionary, typically a large academic one, which sets out to contribute to a complete historical record of the language, and is often intended ultimately to be incorporated into a new edition of its parent dictionary.

Notable examples of this genre include the *Supplement to the Oxford English Dictionary* (1972–85) (subsequently included in the second edition of the OED, 1989) and, from the USA, *12,000 Words* (1986), supplementary to *Webster's Third New International Dictionary* (1961). In contrast to these, we also have independent self-contained dictionaries recording neologisms from a particular delimited period, such as *A Dictionary of New English* (Barnhart, Steinmetz & Barnhart, 1973) and the *Longman Register of New Words* (Ayto, 1989).

This dichotomy determines very different approaches to the monitoring of new vocabulary. The supplementary variety is, like its parent, typically interested in making as nearly exhaustive, comprehensive a record of lexical development in a given period as is possible within its terms of reference. It therefore tends to include among its entries words which are morphologically unremarkable and of minimal semantic interest (some straightforward derivatives of the *nonreflationary* type, for instance) so long as it has sufficient evidence of their use. And since such dictionaries usually regard themselves as more or less permanent records of the language, they apply rather stringent inclusion criteria: their lexicographers will wish to satisfy themselves (using whatever tests they find appropriate) that a new item has established itself in the language before putting it in the dictionary. (However, as online dictionaries and instant updating come more to the fore, this last consideration will probably come to apply progressively less and less.)

The self-contained dictionary of neologisms, however, tends in practice to be more selective in what it includes. It is not tied to the yoke of comprehensiveness, and compilers of such books therefore usually feel themselves free to put to one side potential entries that are formally regular or otherwise of little interest. They are usually not so concerned with durability, either, so they may well allow in nonsense words and idiologisms of the sort that supplementary dictionaries would exclude.

So, in using such dictionaries as sources of data about neologisms, one is not necessarily comparing like with like. To this caveat another needs to be added: no matter how large the dictionary, it can never hope to capture all of the new formations, many of them ephemeral, that are being coined all the time. In the present state of the art this applies particularly to the spoken language, dictionary coverage of which is still fairly weak. In recording the written language, dictionaries may be incomplete but their sampling is probably representative, proportionate to the whole; as far as the spoken language is concerned, we cannot even say this for certain.

That said, what can we learn from dictionaries about the processes of word formation in English? Discussions of this topic tend to focus on the more glamorous types of coinage, such as blends, back-formation, acronyms and totally new creations, and on foreign borrowings. But an analysis of the entries in *6,000 Words* (Cannon, 1978) has shown that the true picture at a bread-and-butter level is vastly different (see Table 6.1).

Table 6.1 An analysis of entries in *6,000 words*

affixation	29.6%	initialisms	3.4%
compounding	28.0%	functional shifts	2.0%
semantic change	18.3%	abbreviations	0.7%
borrowings	6.1%	blends	0.7%
proper-noun derivatives	5.0%	back-formations	0.5%
shortenings	3.6%	coinings & trademarks	0.4%

Well over half of these 'new' lexical items were formed by derivation and compounding — that is, the reshuffling of existing elements — and if we add in semantic change, the development of new meanings in established words, 75% of the total is accounted for. High-profile categories such as acronyms — very popular these days — and coinings (such as *quark* and *ticky-tacky*) make up an insignificant percentage of the total.

Similar analyses of the entries in the *Longman Register of New Words*, Vol. 1 (Ayto, 1989) (see Table 6.2) and the *Macquarie Dictionary of New Words* (Butler, 1990) (see Table 6.3) show broadly similar results.

Table 6.2 An analysis of entries in *Longman Register of New Words*, Vol. 1

compounding	39.8%	shortenings	2.2%
affixation	25.1%	initialisms	1.8%
semantic change	13.2%	back-formations	1.3%
blends	5.1%	proper-noun derivatives	1.3%
functional shifts	3.5%	coinings & trademarks	0.5%
borrowings	3.3%	rhyming slang	0.2%
abbreviations	2.6%		

As can be seen in Table 6.2, compounding, affixation, and semantic change between them once again account for about three-quarters of the total (the proportionally higher score for compounds is probably to be accounted for by the fact that Ayto admits some semantically-transparent compounds of the sort that *6,000 Words* would exclude).

Table 6.3 An analysis of entries in *Macquarie Dictionary of New Words*

compounding	54.5%	abbreviations	2.8%
affixation	15.4%	proper-noun derivatives	2.4%
semantic change	10.3%	initialisms	1.9%
borrowings	3.6%	shortenings	1.1%
functional shifts	3.2%	back-formations	1.0%
blends	2.8%	coinings & trademarks	1.0%

In Table 6.3 there is apparently a substantial weighting in favour of compounds, but in fact this is due to an entry policy that maximises the number of headwords by including separately all minimal variants (*cellular phone, cellular telephone*) and derivatives of the same compound base (*ink-jet printer, ink-jet printing*), and the overall score for the trio of compounding, affixation, and semantic change (80.2%) is not greatly in excess of those of *6,000 Words* and Ayto's *Longman Register of New Words*, Vol. 1.

Another question dictionaries may throw some light on is the durability of new coinages. Clearly, the life expectancy of a neologism entered in a dictionary depends not only on the stringency of the criteria for entering it — the greater the number of recorded occurrences, the greater the likelihood of at least temporary establishment — but also on the rigour with which the lexicographer applies them, which is an imponderable. But that said, it may be of interest to take a section of a dictionary of neologisms (*A Dictionary of New English*, Barnhart, Steinmetz & Barnhart, 1973) and see how many of them survive into a dictionary of general English published 13 years later (*Collins English Dictionary*, 1986). It emerges that of the entries beginning A and B, 167, about a third of the total, have made it. Some of them are obscure or technical terms, but many are very familiar now, for example:

action painting, adventure playground, aerobics, ageism, aggro, ashram, au pair, autocue, baryon, BASIC, behaviour therapy, biathlon, biodegradable, biological clock, biorhythm, bird strike, black box, black hole, black power, block release, boatel, body language, bovver, brain death, breathalyser, brown fat, bummer, buzz word, byte.

Extrapolated over the whole dictionary this would give a figure of about 1,500 new words, which would represent roughly 2% of the entries in a large desk dictionary or perhaps about 3.3% of the average educated person's mental lexicon (cf. Aitchison, this volume). Whatever reservations one may have about the general applicability of these findings, they do at least give some indication of the healthy growth rate of the language.

Finally, of course, neologisms reflect current concerns and trends in society. In particular, they reveal which areas of activity are most fertile in the creating of new vocabulary. In the 1970s, for example, computing was well to the fore, but in the 1980s it was decisively overtaken by the financial world. Analysis of subject areas covered in dictionaries of neologisms of that decade (for example Mort, 1986; Ayto, 1989) reveals that terminology relating to the City of London, share-dealing and various sorts of financial manoeuvring significantly outnumbered all other topics. What is more, many of the coinages display an exuberance of inventiveness lacking in other areas: *Chinese walls, concert parties, dawn raids, dead-cat bounces, fan clubs, golden goodbyes, marzipan layers, mezzanine bonds, platinum handshakes, poison pills, rocket scientists, tin parachutes, white knights* and *white squires* have a surreal poetry of their own. An allied area is the welter of lifestyle acronyms which followed *yuppie* into the language from 1984 onwards: *buppies, puppies, corrupies, guppies, huppies, cuppies* and *juppies*, not to mention all the variants such as *lombards, bobos, dinkies, docknies, pippies* and *whannies* that fell over themselves in an ever-increasing attempt (mainly on the part of journalists, one suspects) to be original and amusing.

However, in October 1987 came the big crash, when stock markets around the world tumbled. Share prices subsequently recovered, but there was a radical shake-out in the financial sector: jobs and confidence were lost and caution reigned. The climate was not propitious for new schemes, so the need for new terminology fell off. The material collected in the late 1980s for Volume 2 of the *Longman Register of New Words* (Ayto, 1990) revealed a dramatic drop in the incidence of financial neologisms.

No other single field can be said to have entirely taken over the lead in lexical productivity in this period, but one of the main front-runners is the environment. The late 1980s saw the transition of ecology from a fringe concern to the stuff of prime-ministerial speeches and government White Papers, and a proliferation of eco-vocabulary in the general language followed. The prefix *eco-* was in the vanguard, being tacked on to all sorts of unlikely-sounding base-forms (*eco-conscious, eco-sound, eco-speak, eco-*

tourism etc.) The adjective *green*, in its environmentalist sense, was also in vogue, providing terms like *green audit, greenery* and *greenism*. And a clear sign that environmentalism had arrived was the appearance of *cruelty-free, eco-labelled, ozone-friendly* and the like on the packaging of consumer goods.

Dedicated dictionaries of neologisms provide an invaluable service to translators, language learners and the like, both in bridging the inevitable time gap between the appearance of new words and their inclusion in standard dictionaries, and in recording ephemeral or rare items that might not even make it into standard dictionaries. At least until the advent of widely-available instantly-updated online dictionaries, and perhaps beyond, they will continue to have a key role to play.

References

AYTO, J. 1989, *Longman Register of New Words* Vol. 1. London: Longman.
— 1990, *Longman of Register of New Words* Vol. 2. London: Longman.
BARNHART, C.L., STEINMETZ, S. and BARNHART, R.K. 1973, *A Dictionary of New English 1963–1972*. London: Longman.
BUTLER, S. 1990, *Macquarie Dictionary of New Words*. Macquarie University, NSW: The Macquarie Library.
CANNON, G. 1978, Review of '6,000 Words'. *Language* 54, 446–8.
Chambers English Dictionary 1988. Edinburgh: Chambers.
Collins English Dictionary 1986. London: Collins.
MORT, S. 1986, *Longman Guardian New Words*. London: Longman.
O'KILL, B. 1988, *Collecting and Using Neologisms*. Paper presented to the EURALEX International Congress, Budapest.
Oxford English Dictionary 2nd edn. 1989. Oxford: Clarendon Press.
6,000 Words: A Supplement to Webster's Third New International Dictionary. 1976. Springfield, MA: Merriam-Webster.
A Supplement to the Oxford English Dictionary. 1972–1985. Oxford: Clarendon Press.
12,000 Words: A Supplement to Webster's Third New International Dictionary. 1986. Springfield, MA: Merriam-Webster.
Webster's Third New International Dictionary of the American Language. 1961. Springfield, MA: Merriam-Webster.

7 Beyond the Dictionary: The Translator, the L2 Learner and the Computer

MARGARET ROGERS

The foreign or second language learner and the translator have a good deal in common when it comes to dealing with words: each must identify new words, record them, learn them, recall them, work out their relationships with other words and with the real world, and be able to use them appropriately. In this chapter, it will be suggested that recent developments in computer-assisted translation can form a useful model for helping L2 learners to perform all of these tasks.

Second language learners frequently find themselves attempting to translate from their mother tongue (L1) into their new second or foreign language (L2), particularly to fill lexical gaps or to locate L2 words which are only dimly recalled. And all translators are in a sense L2 learners, continually extending their knowledge of the languages with which they work, particularly in the area of vocabulary. Established professionals translating into their L1 are unlikely to experience serious grammatical difficulties in understanding the source text (ST) or in producing the target text (TT), but translation problems with vocabulary are not uncommon. Since the majority of texts translated today are special-language (LSP) texts dealing with specialised subject fields, for translators vocabulary problems are usually terminological.

Translation theorists rightly stress that translation is much more than transferring the meaning of words from the ST to the TT (cf. for instance Koller, 1992: 133). But when it comes to discussing the translation of specialist words — or terms — in LSP texts, the difficulties may easily be underestimated, since it is often assumed that equivalence is more easily established than in general language (cf. Newmark, this volume). Coseriu, the well-known Romance linguist, has remarked, for instance, that the international character of many scientific subjects lends itself to a one-to-one relationship between terms in each language (Coseriu, 1975: 28)[1] (cf. also Snell-Hornby (1993), as discussed by Anderman, this volume). More recently the universality of scientific and technical concepts has been convincingly questioned from different perspectives (Schmitt, 1986; Arntz, 1988; Kohn, 1990). The translation of terms in LSP texts therefore poses significant problems, although the particular study of terms and the problems which they raise in translation — translation-oriented terminology — is relatively new.

The lexical problems of L2 learners have been similarly underrated over the years. Much less has been written, for instance, about how they acquire words than about how they acquire grammar. Teaching priorities have reflected this emphasis. But non-native language learners are themselves quick to identify lexical problems as their greatest single source of difficulty, and native speakers are said to find lexical errors 'more disruptive and more serious than grammatical errors' (Meara, 1984: 229). Lexical errors have indeed been shown to outnumber grammatical errors by a wide margin (Cornu, 1979: 262), and researchers have suggested that the richness of learners' vocabulary knowledge is related to the level of academic achievement in second language situations (Saville-Troike, 1984: 216; Verhallen & Schoonen, 1993).

So where can translators and L2 learners seek help with their vocabulary? As far as translators are concerned dictionaries are of some value, although this is limited. On the one hand, their coverage, particularly of fast-growing specialised subject fields, is rarely if ever comprehensive, and on the other hand the conceptual and linguistic information they contain is often sketchy. Specialised bilingual dictionaries, for instance, do not normally contain definitions or examples of contextual use, neither do they distinguish clearly between synonyms in the target language. Nevertheless, translators are encouraged in their training to use dictionaries, albeit from a critical perspective, but to supplement them with many other reference sources.

Dictionary resources are also often inadequate for the special needs of L2 learners, especially for learners of languages other than English. The first learner's dictionary of German — *Langenscheidts Großwörterbuch Deutsch als Fremdsprache* — did not appear until late 1993, nearly half a century after A.S. Hornby's *Learner's Dictionary of Current English* (1948). The pitfalls of bilingual dictionaries, with their impenetrable labels and tempting lists of undifferentiated equivalents, are familiar to any learner who has tried to use them. Against this background, the role of dictionaries in the classroom has been controversial. During the 1960s and 1970s, for instance, they remained out of favour in the L2 classroom — at least in the UK — first in the context of behaviouristic audiolingual methods of teaching, and then in the context of the more recent communicatively-based approach to L2 pedagogy, which stresses the importance of learners' actual use of language as opposed to their knowledge of the language system. And as an attempt to codify aspects of lexical knowledge, the dictionary is part of the system of language, just as a grammar is an attempt to model aspects of the native speaker's knowledge of morphology and syntax.

So where does this leave the dictionary? In this chapter, I would like to look beyond the usual notion of a dictionary as a static alphabetically-ordered list of entries towards a more dynamic kind of lexical resource. The idea is based on recent work concerning the provision of terminology for specialist translators as a part of a 'translator's workbench' (Kugler, Ahmad & Thurmair, 1995). In such a workbench — a set of computer tools to be used as required — it is envisaged that translators have access not only to existing resources such as electronic dictionaries and collections of terms, but also to the means to create their own specialised dictionaries based on authentic texts using dedicated software tools (cf. Ahmad & Rogers, in press).

It seems that similar workbench facilities — a learner's workbench-for-words — could profitably be offered to L2 learners: just as the translator's workbench provides an alternative to the costly and elusive solution of fully-automatic high-quality machine translation, so the L2 learner's workbench may prove to be more flexible and comprehensive than other computer-based solutions to the teaching and learning of vocabulary, such as intelligent computer-assisted language learning.

L2 Learners' Lexical Needs

Since the end of the second world war lexicographical practice has demonstrated an increasing awareness of specialised users' needs, particularly in respect of foreign language learners (Cowie, 1981), and yet the view that dictionaries are a common and obvious aid to various lexical aspects of language learning (Ilson, 1985), as well as for language use, is surprisingly not one which is universally accepted. In an article describing the role of traditional dictionaries in language learning, Summers (1988a: 112) critically notes a prevailing pedagogical view that 'newly encountered words should only be decoded by means of contextual cues', in other words, *not* by reference to a dictionary, but rather by reference to text or situational context.

A further reason why dictionaries may not be favoured as a learning resource concerns the organisation of the lexical material they contain. It has been suggested, for instance, that the information found in alphabetical dictionaries is not sufficient for non-native language learners to build up their mental lexicon. In addition to collecting information (subconsciously) about each lexical item, such as that normally found in alphabetical dictionaries, non-native learners will be 'seeking to make those conceptual links usually only touched on in thesauruses' (Rossner, 1985: 96–7).

The L2 learner also needs information which incorporates variations in uses and meanings according to text type, situation and context. In other words, we can think of the learner needing information on how words interact with their neighbours in text, i.e. syntagmatic relations, what their subordinates or superordinates or equivalents are, i.e. paradigmatic relations, and on what occasions they may be used, i.e. pragmatic aspects. And last but not least there is denotational meaning, by no means a straightforward affair, since each word has a range of potential meanings of which just one aspect may be realised in any particular context. So the concept of 'book' in *I read the book* is not the same 'book' as the ones in *I wrote the book* or *I bound the book*.

But how can language teachers determine what their students' lexical needs actually are and how these might best be met pedagogically? Possible ways of approaching the problem include asking learners themselves or studying their errors. Surveys of advanced foreign learners and users suggest that the meaning of words is the type of information most frequently sought in dictionaries of English, both specialist and general, and that information relevant to production, such as syntactic patterns, is typically consulted much less frequently (Tomaszczyk, 1979; Béjoint, 1981). One survey of students' errors in a writing exercise has drawn attention to the inadequate semantic information in learners' dictionaries, leading to the inappropriate interchange of apparent synonyms (e.g. *conveyance, transport, vehicle*) (Jain, 1981), errors which are also familiar to translators.

Another way to approach the question of learners' needs is to look at how vocabulary is acquired and stored in the mental lexicon. Most studies of the lexicon focus on what we can call 'designative words' (after Zgusta, 1971: 101), i.e. content words, rather than function words. It has been suggested that such words are organised mentally by adult native speakers in semantic fields, e.g. fruits, vehicles, times, animals, and within those fields, linked in a network of associations, as we have seen in previous chapters. Likely candidates for types of link between words include collocation (e.g. *salt water*), coordination (e.g. *salt, pepper, mustard*), superordination (*red, green* and *blue* are *colours*) and synonymy (e.g. *hungry, starved*) (Aitchison, 1994: 84–5). To recap, the links which are thought to have priority are collocation and coordination.

We can study the mental lexicon from a number of perspectives, but the complexity of studying how human beings deal with words grows if we consider that bilinguality is more common than monolinguality, and that various forms and levels of 'bilinguality' are possible (Appel & Muysken, 1987: 2–3; Schreuder & Weltens, 1993: 2–4). Methods used to investigate the bilingual lexicon include, most obviously, translation (Kroll, 1993; Snodgrass, 1993).

So how is the L2 mental lexicon organised and does translation play any part? Meara (1984: 231) suggests that the 'ordering' of items in the L2 mental lexicon is similar to that discussed for L1, and includes 'some sort of semantic-based system, as in a thesaurus'. There is, in fact, according to Aitchison (1994: 236), reason to believe that the occurrence of bilingual blends such as *Springling* (from the English *Spring* and the German *Frühling*) indicates one integrated network for bilingual speakers. Miller and Fellbaum (1992: 91–3) also propose that the most likely model for what they call the 'bilingual lexical matrix' is that of 'concept mediation' between languages, so that words representing the same concept (e.g. English *mother*, German *Mutter*, French *mère*, Swedish *mor*) may be found at the same mental 'address', which is defined by the concept. Some recent research using auditory stimuli in Dutch and English also suggests that the bilingual lexicon is organised in a 'single semantic memory' with 'language-specific tags' (de Bot *et al.*, 1995). Other models of the bilingual lexicon seem less likely, according to Miller and Fellbaum. These include an independent lexical matrix for each language, i.e. each language has its own separate location; and a word-to-word mapping based on a single lexical matrix for the first language, to which words in other languages are added as paired associates. In other words, translation seems to play little or no role in the organisation of the bilingual mental lexicon.

Elsewhere, however, the importance of adopting a dynamic model of the bilingual lexicon has been stressed, allowing for words to enter into different interlingual relations and to establish new interlingual links according to developmental and situational factors (Schreuder & Weltens, 1993: 7; Hulstijn, 1994: 175), including the language direction from L1 to L2, or from L2 to L1. It has been proposed, for instance, that beginning L2 learners translate *into* the L2 by means of direct word association, i.e. translation from L1 to L2, whereas more advanced learners operate by linking the L1 word with the L2 word indirectly through a shared concept, i.e. L1 → concept → L2 (Kroll, 1993: 67; Snodgrass, 1993: 87). It has also been suggested that certain types of training, e.g. for interpreters, may encourage word-for-word retrieval based on a direct link between the L1 word and the L2 word rather than on concept mediation (Hulstijn, 1994: 175).

At the least, it seems reasonable to assume that L2 learners impose some 'intelligible organisation' on the words they learn in order to exercise 'cognitive economy', as do L1 learners (Miller, 1978: 61), and that this organisation is largely semantically based — rather than, say, alphabetically — with some interdependence between the L1 and the L2. Otherwise, it is hard to imagine how large quantities of vocabulary can be retained, individual items successfully and speedily retrieved, and links made efficiently between L1 and L2. The way in which most dictionaries are organised is, however, alphabetical, leading us to question whether this is the most appropriate structure for the L2 user, or indeed for the translator. In terminology science — as opposed to LSP lexicography — it is generally accepted that an alphabetically-based organisation is inappropriate for the presentation of specialised dictionaries or 'terminologies'. What is favoured is a conceptual or 'systematic' organisation which reflects the structure of knowledge in the particular subject field, thereby helping the user — often not a subject specialist — to grasp the relations between concepts and to reconstruct the knowledge encoded by the terms and their relations. Such an organisation means not only that related terms appear close together in the dictionary, but also that in bilingual terminologies translation equivalents may be found at the same conceptual 'address'.

What we do know about the organisation of the L2 mental lexicon suggests, then, that semantic links are important in some way in the storage of lexical knowledge and that semantically-based dictionaries may prove to match learners' needs quite closely, as conceptually-based terminologies have been argued to best serve the needs of their users, including translators. We can now go on to ask whether semantic relations are also important in the growth of lexical knowledge.

Teaching and Learning L2 Vocabulary

Until quite recently, many authors have both noted and lamented the low priority given to vocabulary in L2 pedagogy (Cornu, 1979: 262; Channell, 1981: 116; Carter, 1987: 3; Candlin in Carter & McCarthy, 1988: vii), pointing at the same time, however, to a resurgence of interest in vocabulary teaching beyond the grading and selection of items for inclusion in L2 syllabuses. An oft-cited objective is to redress the balance between vocabulary on the one hand and grammar on the other. Indeed, recent publications have proposed that a learners' syllabus — or parts of it at least — can be lexically based (Willis, 1990, 1994). But what should the basis for vocabulary teaching be?

It has been suggested that in a classroom situation the degree of match between learning materials or environments and the semantic organisation of the lexicon is likely to be important for the relative success of the learner in acquiring vocabulary (Cornu, 1979: 264; Esser & Harnisch, 1980: 162–3; Aitchison, 1992: 82; Miller & Fellbaum, 1992: 95; Swartz, 1992: 220). Reflecting this view of a semantically-structured L2 lexicon, Meara (1992) makes a plea for a method of studying L2 vocabulary acquisition which looks at the overall structure of vocabularies rather than at small sets of individual words and meanings. His proposal is to use 'graph theory', a way of representing connections between objects ('points') as a network (or 'graph') in mathematics, as a means of modelling the mental lexicon. Meara sets his subjects — ten advanced non-native speakers of Spanish — a word association task in Spanish (L2) and in English (L1). The subjects' task is to get from the first word in a given random pair to the second by creating a chain of associations between them, e.g. *oven–hot–desert–Arab–veil* (Meara, 1992: 67). Meara hypothesised that L2 learners would produce longer chains than native speakers, since L2 learners could be expected to have fewer connections between words in their lexicon. In fact, this turned out not to be the case for the learners in Meara's study: the L2 Spanish chains were actually shorter than the L1 English chains. A comparison of the L2 Spanish data with parallel L1 Spanish data, however, reveals that the advanced L2 learners in Meara's study behaved in a similar way to L1 speakers of Spanish, suggesting, according to Meara, that the differences lie in the size or organisation of vocabulary in English and Spanish rather than between the L1 and L2 lexicons.

Meara's results are consistent with the claim that advanced L2 learners do not access the L2 via the L1 (cf. Kroll, 1993; Snodgrass, 1993): had this been the case, we would have expected the mean chain lengths between the L2 Spanish words and between the L1 English words to be the same for the same subjects. But as we have seen, this was not the case.

Pursuing the graph metaphor, there is some evidence to suggest that learners do perform better on L2 vocabulary recall tasks if material is presented to them in graph rather than list form, and if the recall tasks are also performed using graphs (Esser & Harnisch, 1980). A graph can be understood here as a map of relations between concepts, e.g. ACTOR; INSTRUMENT; PLACE, and of relations characterising individual concepts, e.g. IS, HAS, CAN, IS A. Each concept is labelled with a word. Esser and Harnisch (1980: 163) show how a *shark* IS A *fish* and a *fish* IS AN *animal* which HAS the properties: IS *animate*, HAS a *metabolism* and CAN *perceive*. All the properties of the concept *animal* are inherited by concepts lower in the hierarchy (*fish* and *shark*). Esser and Harnisch suggest that this kind of organisation has a higher degree of psychological relevance for the mental lexicon than, for instance, pictorial representations of meaning (1980: 163).

Their suggestion is supported by the results of their bilingual vocabulary experiment with adult students of English as L2 with what appears to be German as their L1. The students were tested on their recall of L1–L2 equivalents which had previously been presented to them in a number of ways, including a graph and various kinds of word list, semantically or syntactically structured, or unstructured. Their recall of the L2 English words was then tested by using one of the word lists or the graph format. The results showed that recall was best for those students who both learnt and recalled the words through graphs (36.7%), and worst for those who learnt and recalled the word through unstructured lists (6.3%). Similar conclusions about the value of associative networks for the recall of vocabulary items have also been suggested for advanced adult English learners of French (Swartz, 1992). Assuming that Esser and Harnisch's claim about the psychological relevance of the graph configuration for the mental lexicon is correct, then their results suggest that a correspondence between method of presentation and psychological organisation facilitates learning.

In their book on learner language, Færch, Haastrup & Phillipson (1984) attempt to relate the structure of the learner's 'interlanguage vocabulary' to vocabulary teaching. Interestingly, their perspective differs from that of other authors, who suggest that the structure of the mental lexicon should influence teaching strategies: Færch *et al.* propose that the teaching method has a conditioning effect on the structure of the learner's interlanguage vocabulary. In other words, they indicate that the pattern of the teaching shapes the pattern of learning and organisation for the learner. So, for instance, if we follow their proposal, interlanguage vocabulary will be structured according to whether the L2 vocabulary is taught by relating it to L1 vocabulary, e.g. by translation, or by reference to other L2 words, e.g. by synonyms, antonyms, hyponyms. Some tentative support for Færch *et al.*'s point of view may be found in the experimental literature, where the teaching of L2 equivalents by word-for-word translation with beginning learners is considered as a possible influence on the way in which L2 words are retrieved from semantic memory, i.e. by L1-word-for-L2-word association rather than through concept mediation (Snodgrass, 1993: 87).

Traditionally, much vocabulary teaching, at least with linguistically-homogeneous groups of learners, has indeed relied on presenting students with bilingual vocabulary lists to learn, referring to equivalent or near-equivalent L1 words (cf. Carter & McCarthy, 1988: 12-3 for a discussion of lists and memorisation; also Meara, this volume). Even when teaching relies on other means, such as monolingual exercises in some kind of context, it is my experience that students still tend to keep bilingual lists for their own private learning and for future reference. Notwithstanding students' own organisational preferences, the pedagogical literature of the 1980s and 1990s suggests a move towards a much richer set of presentation strategies than such lists, at least in L2 English-language teaching, particularly for intermediate and advanced learners. However, individual preferences in ways of learning vocabulary need to be taken into account in determining pedagogical strategies, as does the closeness of the linguistic relationship between the L1 and the L2 (Meara, 1993: 285, 288-9). As Meara indicates, there is little point, for instance, in concentrating on basic vocabulary in an L2 which shares many cognates in the same high frequency band with the learner's L1. Surprisingly, what Meara calls this 'latent' vocabulary remains unexploited in most foreign language courses (1993: 282).

It is now almost a commonplace to say that good foreign or second language teaching is optimally related to our knowledge of how learners learn, even though it is by no means obvious how knowledge of learning can optimally inform pedagogical strategies. This is not a new observation in the pedagogy of vocabulary (cf. Cornu, 1979: 264, 272; Channell, 1981: 117; Carter & McCarthy, 1988: 11), but it is certainly not one which is always put into practice. For instance, in a recent publication entitled *Teaching and Learning Vocabulary* (Taylor, 1990), information specifically on L2 vocabulary *learning* is hard to find. So we can only conclude that the advice on *teaching* is based on other information, in other words on principles motivated from elsewhere, such as sociolinguistic concepts, e.g. communicative competence; or semantic theory, e.g. semantic fields, componential analysis, collocational analysis; or on experience, i.e. what has worked in the past. This is not to say that such advice lacks interest — simply that it is not informed by some knowledge of how L2 vocabulary is learned, stored and retrieved.

Nevertheless, two of the organisational principles suggested for the mental lexicon, namely semantic fields and collocations, are reflected in certain pedagogical techniques described by McCarthy (1990). The use of 'semantic maps' as a means of organising vocabulary is one example which is discussed by McCarthy in this way (1990: 95-6). Such maps, which share certain features with the graphs discussed earlier, are comprised of items of vocabulary, referred to as 'nodes', and relations of various kinds (IS A, HAS, DOES, IS, EXAMPLE) which may also assign attributes to the nodes themselves, e.g. *dog* DOES *bark*; *dog* IS *loyal*; *dog* HAS *teeth*; *dog* HAS *hair*; *dog* IS *carnivorous*. As an illustration of how a semantic map can be used in the classroom, McCarthy reports on a vocabulary exercise in which learners can themselves draw a very loose kind of graph in order to organise the vocabulary of a particular topic according to their own personal associations. The example reported shows how a learner builds up a freely-structured associative network of vocabulary items in the field of politics. At the centre is the word *politics* itself. Directly associated with it are *politician, parliament, policy* and *political parties*. Associated with each of these words is a further set. For example, attached to *parliament* are two expressions: *House of Commons* and *House of Lords*. These then share the expression *ratify laws*. A further chain starts from *House of Commons* leading to *ministers* and then to *civil service*. The network, as McCarthy points out, is really a map of the learner's encyclopaedic knowledge. As with Esser and Harnisch's graphs (1980), it incorporates links of equivalence, association and hierarchy: the *Prime Minister* IS A *politician*; the *Member of Parliament* HAS a *constituency*; a *left wing political party* IS A KIND OF *political party*.

Such relations of association, equivalence and hierarchy also characterise the organisation of terms in concept-based terminologies (cf. for instance Picht & Draskau, 1985: 62–117). In a conceptual organisation, terms which are semantically associated with each other in some way are presented to the user joined by some kind of link, often based on a system of subject classification. Such an organisation is particularly helpful to translators, who may use it to supplement their own, perhaps non-expert, knowledge of the subject field. In other words, it provides encyclopaedic knowledge.

The technological means to represent the relations between concepts and the words which represent them is already available in the form of computerised tools to create 'conceptual graphs', also as a part of a translator's workbench (cf. Hook & Ahmad, 1992). These graphs are more than a computer copy of a manual graph: the system 'knows' something about the concepts it represents, allowing connections to be made between concepts which facilitate retrieval by the user. The system can, for instance, find the nearest match where a particular concept is missing from the graph. Conceptual graphs allow concepts to be organised in flexible configurations, reflecting the fact that words may take on different senses in different semantic fields, even though the object of reference is physically constant. For instance, *dog* may be a 'pet', as are *cat* and *goldfish*, but *dog* may also be a 'guard' alongside *burglar alarm* and *goose* (Dunbar, 1991: 37–8). For translators, grouping terms together according to subject field may also help to avoid translation errors arising from patterns of polysemy in the source language which do not match those in the target language. In English, for instance, the same word form *bridge* is used to refer to the arch of the nose, the device used to cover a gap between teeth in the mouth, and the wooden device supporting the strings on a musical instrument. In German, a different term is required in each case: *Sattel* (anatomy); *Brücke* (dentistry); *Steg* (music). And even within a single semantic field, individuals may choose to organise the lexical items in different sets of relations, depending on the organising characteristics chosen, or simply because each person's mental lexicon is different (cf. Rivers, 1983: 127). A reasonable conclusion is therefore that learners should be given the means to create their own graphs in order to represent the associations between words.

Following the use of graphs to represent semantic fields, collocation, i.e. the regular occurrence of words together in text, is another kind of semantic relationship which often features in vocabulary teaching (McCarthy, 1990: 98; Taylor, 1990: 24) and now also in dictionaries designed for advanced learners (e.g. Benson, Benson & Ilson, 1986).

Collocation exercises are designed to help learners, often at an intermediate or advanced level, to combine words according to typical native-speaker patterns. Similarly, translators using a special language specific to a particular subject field need to learn appropriate collocational patterns, since these are not necessarily predictable from general language, often being highly restricted. The types of collocation which are of interest for L2 learners may be lexical collocations — compare *impeccable taste* (OK), *immaculate taste* (possibly), and *spotless taste* (not OK) — or grammatical collocations — compare *by accident* (OK) and *from accident* (not OK), and *afraid of* (OK) and *afraid before* (not OK). For translators, even when translating into their L1, LSP collocations may prove problematic since collocational patterns are often not transferable across languages. When translating from Danish to English, for instance, in the field of automotive engineering, the translator must know that there are different translations for the verb *engage* depending on its collocate. Hence, when combined with *clutch* (*to engage the clutch*), the translation is *slippe* (*slippe koblingen*); when combined with *brake*, the translation is *træde på* (*træde på bremsen*); and when combined with *handbrake*, the translation is different again, *trække* (*trække håndbremsen*).[2] Such patterns can be found in texts but are rarely codified in LSP dictionaries in a systematic way. Access to a corpus of texts is therefore of benefit to translators seeking to find the appropriate collocation, particularly if searches are automated as in a translator's workbench. L2 learners might also benefit from the same facility.

In this section we have looked at some of the concerns of L2 vocabulary teaching, particularly in relation to English-language teaching, which is the most well documented. We have also seen how certain methods of semantic presentation and problems of collocational behaviour are of equal concern to translators, and that certain technological solutions are available in this context.

Let us now turn to the reference works that attempt to codify lexical meaning. We will focus our attention on those 'dictionaries' where meaning serves as an organising principle in some way in order to assess the value of these resources for their users.

Dictionaries as Models of Lexical Knowledge

According to Zgusta (1971: 21): 'Lexical meaning stands in the center of the lexicographer's attention'. Meaning may also be central for non-native users of dictionaries (Summers, 1988b: 11), and, in its many guises from word to sentence to text, may be viewed as central to translation. But it is well known among lexicographers that the representation of meaning in dictionaries is inconsistent, incomplete and unsystematic in a number of respects (Atkins, 1991: 168; Boguraev, 1991: 228; Levin, 1991: 206). As these writers point out, it is the age of the machine-readable dictionary which has focused attention on these and other representational problems. Dictionaries are valuable repositories of lexical knowledge, but they are insufficiently rich to serve as an online resource to which natural language processing systems may refer. While human readers are able to interpret and supplement dictionary entries from their knowledge about the general properties of language, as well as from their knowledge about the world, computers have no such knowledge and therefore require a much higher degree of explicitness and consistency in order to interpret the information which is represented. To a certain extent, translators find themselves in a similar position of requiring greater explicitness than even monolingual specialised dictionaries usually provide, possibly because these have been compiled with subject experts in mind, i.e. users who can fill in the gaps and resolve the inconsistencies from their subject knowledge and from their experience of writing in the relevant special language.

Foreign learners may also experience difficulties in interpreting dictionary entries in so far as they need far more explicit information than native speakers, particularly about relations between words. As Boguraev (1991: 240) points out, a 'localist' approach to building the semantic component of a computational lexicon or a 'lexical knowledge base' (1991: 227) which focuses on individual entries or small sets of entries, misses generalisations about 'global lexical organisation'. Zgusta has also stressed the importance within 'manual' lexicography of 'survey[ing] groups of semantically related words as wholes' (1971: 103), as did Meara (1992) in his discussion of how to investigate the L2 lexicon using graphs.

Indeed, attempts have been made in both general-purpose and special-purpose lexicography to capture some of the complexity of the lexicon along semantic lines, in most cases independently of the requirement for explicitness necessary for machine-readable dictionaries. In what follows we consider the following kinds of publication: thesauri, collocational dictionaries, and electronic or machine-readable dictionaries, with a view to assessing their role in presenting aspects of meaning to L2 learners.

Thesauri

Thesauri are basically of two kinds: the lexicographical thesaurus, in which general language vocabulary is organised from a semantic point of view; and the documentation thesaurus, a tool for the indexing and retrieval of information within specific fields of knowledge. We are concerned here only with the first type of linguistically-oriented thesaurus.

The best-known thesaurus is *Roget's Thesaurus*. It is 'essentially a collection of words and phrases classified according to underlying concepts and meanings' (Kirkpatrick, Preface to the 1987 edition), originally intended as an aid to writing, including translation (Introduction to the first edition, 1852). It is characterised by the abstract nature of its classification system, which includes at the top level 'abstract relations'; 'space'; 'matter'; 'intellect'; 'volition'; 'emotion', 'religion' and 'morality'. Semantically-related words are simply listed, grouped together according to word class, having been classified according to further subdivisions of the main classification system. It is clear that the profitable use of such a resource requires considerable skill and prior knowledge, since the user must distinguish between close and distant synonyms, establish register, distinguish common and rare words, match collocations and so on.

Attempts have also been made in German to produce general-purpose dictionaries on semantic principles, notably Hallig and von Wartburg's (1952) conceptual system which was intended as a basis for lexicographical work — *Begriffssystem als Grundlage für die Lexikographie. Versuch eines Ordnungsschemas*, and Dornseiff's (1970) German vocabulary according to subject fields: *Der deutsche Wortschatz nach Sachgruppen*.

While such attempts to represent the organisation of vocabulary according to its 'meaning' avoid the semantic arbitrariness of alphabetical and word-based organisation, they in their turn have also been criticised.

Lyons (1977: 300), for instance, criticises Hallig and von Wartburg's claim that their conceptual system is empirically based and universal, reflecting the 'intelligent average person's view of the world', by pointing out that it actually favours 'the naive realism of speakers of what Whorf [...] called Standard Average European'.

Such differences in perspective and attitude are not only to be found synchronically. If we compare the classification system used in a recent thesaurus of the 1980s with that adopted by Roget in the mid-nineteenth century, and largely retained in subsequent editions, we can see a major reorientation, indicating a changed view of the world across time. McArthur's (1981) *Longman Lexicon of Contemporary English* has at the top level of classification fourteen categories, including 'life and living things'; 'the body'; 'people and the family'; 'food, drink and farming'; 'feelings, emotions, attitudes and sensations'; and so on. In addition, the *Longman Lexicon* gives simple definitions of words, pragmatic information (e.g. formal; pompous) and contextual examples, as well as some limited grammatical information. This 'lexicon' is therefore a thesaurus which contains information beyond the classification of words according to meaning.

A more recent attempt to present lexical data to learners in a semantically-based organisation can be found in the *Longman Language Activator* (Rudman, 1993), in which 1052 'concepts' or 'keywords' are the basic entry units, organised alphabetically but providing what is said to be a 'concept map of English'. Each keyword is cross-referenced to other keywords, and distinguished according to its senses, synonyms and definitions. For example, the concept/keyword THIN is divided into three main 'meanings' (related to people, objects or materials, and distance from one side to the other). For each meaning, further distinctions are made; so with regard to people, 'thin in an attractive way' (*slim, slender, trim* etc.) is distinguished from 'thin in a way that is not attractive' (*skinny, scrawny, scraggy* etc.). Illustrative examples are also provided.

Such dictionaries offer practical and relevant help to learners, but lay no claim to have uncovered the key to conceptual universality, which is at best elusive and at worst ill-conceived. Just as lexicographers have different ways of looking at the world, so also might L2 learners show different semantic preferences in their organisation of vocabulary items.

Collocational dictionaries

It has been suggested that the memorisation of a large stock of 'lexicalised units' can be related to fluency in discourse, and that knowledge of such 'multiword units' or collocations may therefore play an important role in a communicative syllabus (Cowie, 1992). Against the background of a growing awareness that recurrent word combinations form a large part of the vocabulary learning load in a foreign or second language, dictionaries dedicated to collocations are now beginning to appear (Mel'cuk, 1984, 1988, 1992; Mel'cuk & Zholkovsky, 1984; Benson, Benson & Ilson, 1986; Kjellmer, 1994). Such dictionaries may be intended for learners themselves (e.g. Benson, Benson & Ilson, 1986) or for researchers, teachers and course writers (e.g. Kjellmer, 1994). Collocation dictionaries may also, of course, be intended for native speakers, such as the *Stilwörterbuch* in the Duden series for German (Drosdowski, 1988), as well as providing valuable help to the translator regarding general language patterns. As we have seen, LSP dictionaries, whether monolingual or bilingual, rarely give collocational patterns, leaving the translator to search elsewhere, e.g. in texts relating to the subject field in question.

Looking at the problem facing non-native speakers from a contrastive perspective, it has been suggested that only those lexical collocations need to be taught which lack translational equivalence (Bahns, 1993). Accordingly, no mention need be made for German learners of English of the verb–noun collocation *to break a promise* (cf. German *ein Versprechen brechen*), while *to keep a promise* (cf. German *ein Versprechen halten* = 'to hold a promise') needs to be pointed out. While such an approach seems economical and well motivated from a pedagogical point of view, it nevertheless assumes that collocational patterns can be translated directly into the L2 given no indication to the contrary. Furthermore, the contrastive approach presupposes linguistically-homogeneous groups of learners. Collocational dictionaries may help to fill this gap, but learners need to be aware that translational equivalence is not necessarily the norm. Access to supplementary materials provides learners with the possibility to test hypotheses, e.g. by examining texts for themselves. As we shall see, it is possible for both translators and learners to search automatically for collocational patterns in text.

Electronic dictionaries

A number of authors have indicated that electronic dictionaries may have advantages over manual dictionaries for foreign learners (Hill, 1985; Kipfer, 1987; Summers, 1988b). The reasons given range from increased 'space' to allow for more detailed and additional information per entry, integration of multimedia channels, to links with back-up corpora, and so on. But while electronic dictionaries which are more or less an electronic replication of a paper-based publication may offer improved search and retrieval possibilities, they are still word-based rather than meaning-based.

The type of electronic dictionary which Boguraev prefers to call 'computer lexicon' or 'lexical knowledge base' can be exemplified here by the WordNet system (Miller & Fellbaum, 1992), which is described as an 'online lexical database for English based on psycholinguistic principles'. WordNet is semantically organised and is based on the idea that lexical knowledge is mentally organised in an associative network. The principal means of representing meaning is through so-called 'synsets' — sets of synonyms — each of which is defined as that set of words which can express the same concept. Further semantic relations, including antonymy, hyponymy, i.e. species–genus, and meronymy, i.e. part–whole, may be created between 'synsets' in the database. In a true concept-based system the option to search according to the intrinsic characteristics of the concept would be given, e.g. 'find me the name of the thing which is a kind of boat and which is flat-bottomed and which travels on canals and rivers' (*barge*). Another way of viewing this would be: how do I get from the definition, or aspects of it, to the word or term? But this appears not to be possible in WordNet.

While electronic dictionaries may provide a useful lexical exploration tool, for L2 learners there are still a number of assumptions which require further investigation. Perhaps the most important of these is the assumption that simply browsing through a monolingual semantic network of the L2 will facilitate acquisition, as suggested by the authors of WordNet (Miller & Fellbaum, 1992: 98). Recall that the learner's active involvement in the creation of networks features strongly in certain pedagogical techniques, and that browsing through a conceptual dictionary may therefore need to be supplemented by the creation of the learner's own networks.

It seems then that semantically-based dictionaries — both conceptually based and collocational — may go some way towards meeting learners' needs, and that computers may play a useful role in this by providing greater opportunities for learners themselves not only to explore lexical patterns but also to make their own lexica.

Turning to Technology

Solutions to pedagogical problems have often been sought optimistically in technology. The use of technology in foreign language teaching has taken various forms through the twentieth century, from the gramophone record and the tape recorder on. While the 1960s and 1970s were the decades of the language laboratory, the 1980s saw the wide-scale introduction of the computer into language teaching, hence computer-assisted language learning, or CALL. As the 1980s progressed, interest in the research community reached beyond what were often simply computerised versions of the earlier fashion for 'programmed learning' books, towards more autonomous 'intelligent' programs, i.e. intelligent computer-assisted language learning, ICALL.

I would like to discuss two possible ways in which learners could be supported in their vocabulary learning by computer programs. The first idea is ICALL; the second — my preferred solution — is a workbench-for-words, integrating the ideas which have been presented so far in this chapter, following the model of the translator's workbench.

ICALL systems

ICALL systems typically consist of three core modules: the state of the learner's knowledge, the pedagogical knowledge of the teacher, and knowledge of the domain (cf. Fox *et al.*, 1992: 67–86 for an overview). Such systems present exciting possibilities beyond earlier rather rigid and behaviouristic CALL programs, but are notoriously difficult to design and implement. Problems include parsing and analysing learners' errors; modelling the learning process; defining the relationship between the teaching and the learning modules; scheduling the teaching strategies; representing the natural-language data to be learnt; and so on. Two systems which are viewed as belonging to the ICALL genre will be briefly considered here: LEXNET-INSITU and SWIM.

LEXNET-INSITU has been developed by Swartz and her colleagues to help American military intelligence linguists retain and use French vocabulary more easily. It is described as a 'discovery learning environment for vocabulary learning' and has no formal tutoring rules (Swartz, 1992: 219). The vocabulary in question belongs mainly to the word class noun (with some verbs) and has a coverage of 166 entries, with semantic and syntactic information associated with each entry (Swartz, 1992: 225). The system uses two kinds of knowledge representation: an associative network for word meanings and a propositional network structure for knowledge of words in discourse. The system has five 'instructional modules' (Swartz, 1992: 225–8), which present and test lexical knowledge; an attempt to 'model people's semantic memory' is explicitly acknowledged (Swartz *et al.*, 1990: 51). Although promising in some ways, Swartz's system has a very limited quantitative coverage of vocabulary items in relation to the effort invested in the design and implementation of the system.

The second system, SWIM (See What I Mean), aims to be a user-driven system for learning how to produce French sentences (Zock, 1992). The system is intended *inter alia* to address the learner's problem of asking 'How do I say X?' where 'X' is a concept for which the form, i.e. the word or expression, is unknown in the L2; the learner therefore needs to get from the concept to the word. The proposed solution to the conceptual problem turns out to be disappointing: learners are simply provided with pre-stored lists of verbs and nouns from which they have to choose, so the system turns out to be word-based rather than concept-based.

The ICALL systems considered here demonstrate not only that the lexical coverage of such systems may be meagre, but also that solutions to fundamental problems of access may be trivial. So solutions need to be sought elsewhere.

A workbench-for-words

A brief consideration of the requirements for ICALL systems has shown what an ambitious enterprise the development of such systems is (cf. Rogers & Ahmad, 1990 for a critical assessment of further ICALL systems). The proposal here for a workbench-for-words is modest in that it assumes no particular teaching or learning model. It allows users/learners to browse and explore databases, dictionaries and texts without imposing a particular structure on the search, and to create their own stores of vocabulary in a database or an associative network. The coverage of such an environment would, however, vastly exceed that of dedicated ICALL systems. So what kinds of tools might our workbench-for-words offer to the user/learner?

A core workbench might contain the following: running text (corpora), electronic dictionaries and encyclopaedia; text-processing tools; a database and a graph-building facility for vocabulary storage and retrieval; database browsing and editing tools; and a word-processing package. In addition, our workbench would offer a management tool for the teacher to add and delete texts and dictionaries and other resources, as well as an authoring package which could be used to design and distribute exercises as required. The tools which are set out on the workbench should be available for use individually or in certain combinations. So, for instance, users should be able to cut and paste material from running text into the database in order to create their own vocabularies; dictionaries and running text should be accessible from exercise files if required; and so on.

The idea of a 'workbench' as a set of integrated computer tools to be used according to need is becoming familiar in the fields of translation (Kugler, Ahmad & Thurmair, 1995), terminology (Holmes-Higgin & Ahmad, 1992), lexicography (Clear, 1993), and language for special purposes (Johnsen & Buhl, 1993).

Text-processing tools

The potential value of running text as a resource for L2 learners has been recognised for some time (Ahmad, Corbett & Rogers, 1985), although the software to process text in a classroom environment using non-mainframe hardware has been slow in following. Two recent examples for English are the Oxford MicroConcord and the Longman Mini Concordancer. The University of Surrey has developed its own text-processing tool — KonText — which operates multilingually with a range of basic functions allowing the user to produce indexes, wordlists, concordances, collocations and frequency-based information. There are many options to allow sorting according to various criteria, to exclude sets of words from searches, to transfer data directly to a database, as well as options for more automatic processing, including statistical computations. KonText is a tool within System Quirk, a workbench designed and implemented to process text and to store and manage this information (Holmes-Higgin *et al.*, 1993)[3]. Its main use to date has been to compile terminologies of special subject fields, including bilingual terminologies, based on structured corpora of text. The data gleaned from the corpora include not only the terms themselves, but also semantic information such as definitions, collocational patterns, synonyms and equivalents, as well as pragmatic information such as variants and their use (Ahmad & Rogers, 1992). Such a facility makes it possible for translators to build their own glossaries and to fill the conceptual and linguistic gaps left by published dictionaries.

It has been suggested that 'the best way to learn the lexicon is to be familiar with a wide range of text' (Gass & Selinker, 1994: 288, referring to Becker, 1991). Corpus material may be useful to L2 learners in a number of ways. Dictionaries indicate what *is* possible through the use of grammatical and stylistic codes, and through the limited use of examples. What they fail to indicate is what is *not* possible. Nor can they fully convey the full potential meaning of a word, which becomes evident from meeting it in a range of linguistic contexts. A corpus will enable the user to see many more examples than the dictionary contains, and, while not solving the problem of negative evidence, will increase the learner's confidence about what is possible, what is typical, what is peripheral, and so on. Learners may also use the corpus to test their intuitions, treating it as a source of evidence about what they think might be the case, where the dictionary fails to answer their questions. Such questions might be of a grammatical nature, e.g. agreement patterns for collective nouns in English, or semantic, e.g. lexical collocations, or simply orthographic, e.g. hyphenation of compounds. Suggestions for exercises using concordances in English can be found in Tribble & Jones (1990).

Electronic dictionaries and encyclopaedias

A number of dictionaries are already available for use on personal computers, sometimes in connection with a CD-ROM drive (e.g. *Collins On-line Bilingual Dictionaries*; *Harrap's Multilingual Dictionary* on CD-ROM; *Le Robert Electronique* on CD-ROM; *Oxford English Dictionary* on CD-ROM). The *Encyclopaedia Britannica* is also available on CD-ROM. And multimedia CDs may provide models for the phonological form of words and expressions. In the future it is to be expected that most dictionaries will be published in electronic as well as paper form.

Vocabulary storage and retrieval

Although translators are increasingly using databases to record terminology for future reference, storing vocabulary in a database is not a widespread practice among L2 learners, even among advanced learners who have regular access to a computer. The idea of the learner's workbench is to offer an integrated database facility to record information when encountered in text or in dictionaries, and to recall information according to need. Databases dedicated to the storage and retrieval of lexical data are in fact now commercially available,[4] usually in the form of so-called 'terminology management software' designed with translators in mind. Since such systems are already designed to accommodate textual data and to cope with bilingual sets of data, they are also relevant to L2 learners' needs.

A more innovative means of storing and retrieving aspects of lexical data which is not yet commercially available is conceptual graphs, mentioned earlier. A tool for building conceptual graphs is available as a part of System Quirk (GraphEd).

Overview

The proposed workbench — based on the modular idea of a translator's workbench — can be viewed as a collection of *tools* which allow the learner to explore *sources* in order to complete *exercises* and to store the *outputs* of those searches in repositories for future reference and modification. As Figure 7.1 shows, the three components of an ICALL system are present —

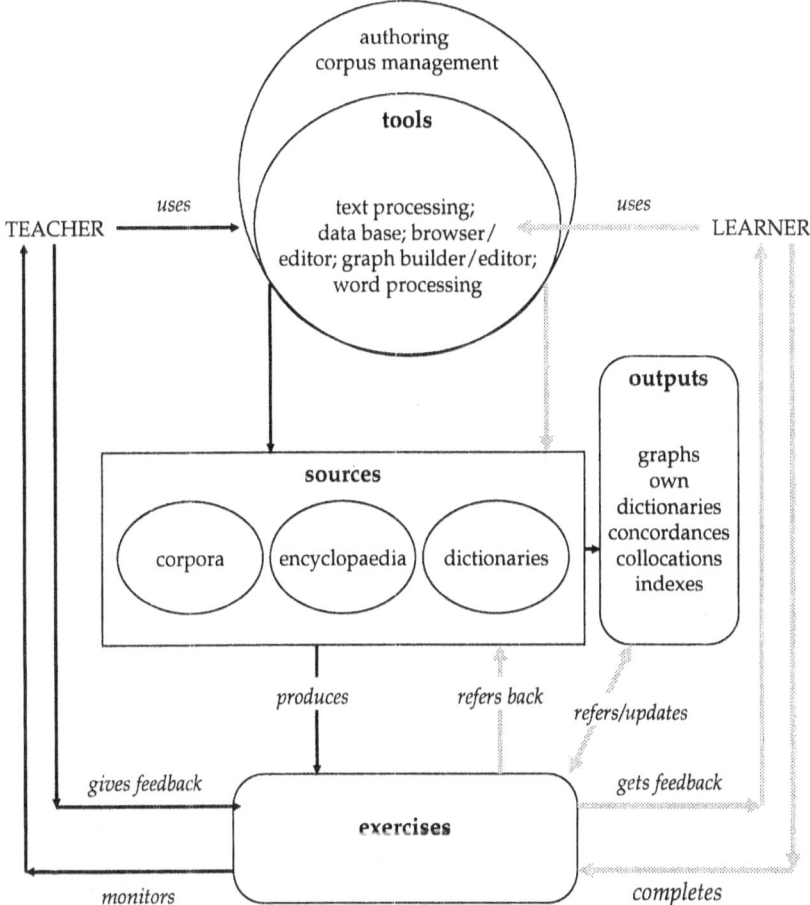

Figure 7.1 A proposal for a workbench-for-words

the teacher, the learner and the expertise module — except that no modelling is required: it is the teacher, not the system, who makes pedagogical decisions; the learner has considerable autonomy to create his or her own patterns of exploration and representation; and the natural-language sources, including texts, dictionaries and encyclopaedic sources, do not have to be interpreted by the system, since they are interpretable by both teacher and learner alike with the aid of software tools.

Conclusion

The investment of costly resources is a *sine qua non* for the development of any computer-assisted learning program, especially if it aims to be 'intelligent'. In this chapter a proposal has been put forward for an L2 learning environment for vocabulary which might be described, in keeping with Fox *et al.*'s suggestion (1992: 83), as 'cognitive CALL' rather than ICALL. The concept of a learner's workbench would obviate the need for automatic error-parsing and pedagogical feedback, while particular tools on the workbench, such as a conceptually-based dictionary, could serve as an expert module.

The workbench concept is also pedagogically consistent with ideas on learner autonomy and the trend to individualisation and self-management in language learning (cf. for instance Carter & McCarthy, 1988: 48; Meara, 1993: 288–9), which is also said to improve students' retention of vocabulary (McCarthy, 1990: 130). Using Halliday's concept of the 'means to mean', Rivers (1983: 124, 127) has argued that L2 learners should be given help in analysing their own 'meanings', noting also that 'students have very personal semantic networks'. In a learning environment such as the proposed workbench-for-words, L2 learners would have the opportunity to devise their own ways of solving a range of comprehension and production problems, as well as dealing with the organisation of vocabulary items for future recall or reference.

Just as fully-automatic high-quality translation is still a distant and elusive goal, so is a fully-automated pedagogical system for language learners. And so it makes sense for L2 learners to benefit from the flexibility of a lexical workbench, as translators may also do, using similar tools for a different but related purpose. The proposal for a learner's workbench-for-words is an attempt to suggest how a user-driven environment might be provided which is exploratory and creative, and ultimately open-ended.

Notes

1. 'Sie [Terminologien] zeichnen sich häufig durch ihre inhaltliche und teilweise sogar formale Zwischensprachlichkeit aus, die durch die Internationalität der betrefffenden Wissenschaften begründet ist. Sie können daher ohne Schwierigkeiten übersetzt werden, sofern die terminologischen Konventionen der betreffenden Sprachen übereinstimmen, denn die Übersetzung bedeutet in diesem Fall nur die Ersetzung eines 'signifiant' durch einen anderen im Verhältnis 1: 1; das 'signifié' bleibt dabei unberührt.' (Coseriu, 1975: 28)
2. The examples are taken from a talk given by Arnt Lykke Jakobsen, Handelshøjskolen i København, entitled 'Translating between English and Danish —

Pitfalls and Problems', at the 10th Conference for Teachers of Scandinavian Studies held at the University of Surrey, Guildford, 10–12 April 1995.
3. This work has been conducted under the auspices of three European Commission ESPRIT-funded projects: Translator's Workbench I (ESPRIT 2315: April 1989-March 1992); Translator's Workbench II (ESPRIT 6005: April 1992-September 1994); Multilex (ESPRIT 5304: December 1990-November 1993). The University of Surrey has participated in all three projects. The System Quirk workbench was developed by Paul Holmes-Higgin, together with Stephen Hook, Stephen Griffin and Syed Sibte Raza Abidi.
4. Some examples covering a range of functionalities are: Aquila; INK TextTools; KeyTerm; Lexbase; Multiterm; TerMs; Term-PC; Termex; Twin; Wordstore 2 (also in French and German: *En tous sens* and *Wortbank*).

References

AHMAD, K., CORBETT, G. and ROGERS, M. 1985, Using computers with advanced language learners: an example. *The Language Teacher* 9/3, 4–7.
AHMAD, K. and ROGERS, M. 1992, Terminology management: A corpus-based approach. In R. TURNER (ed.) *Translating and the Computer 14: Quality, Standards and the Implementation of Technology* (pp. 33–44). London: ASLIB.
— in press, The analysis of text corpora for the creation of advanced terminology databases. In S-E. WRIGHT and G. BUDIN (eds) *Handbook of Terminology Management*. Amsterdam/Philadelphia: John Benjamins.
AITCHISON, J. 1992, Good birds, better birds and amazing birds: The development of prototypes. In P.J.L. ARNAUD and H. BEJOINT (eds) *Vocabulary and Applied Linguistics* (pp. 71–84). Basingstoke: Macmillan.
— 1994, *Words in the Mind: An Introduction to the Mental Lexicon* 2nd edn. Oxford: Blackwell.
APPEL, R. and MUYSKEN, P. 1987, *Language Contact and Bilingualism*. London: Edward Arnold.
ARNTZ, R. 1988, Contrastive terminology work and the training of translators. In G.M. ANDERMAN and M.A. ROGERS (eds) *Translation Studies: State of the Art* (Vol. I of the Proceedings of a Conference held at the University of Surrey, July 1986) (pp. 23–44). Guildford: University of Surrey.
ATKINS, B.T.S. 1991, Building a lexicon: The contribution of lexicography. *International Journal of Lexicography* Special Issue on Building a Lexicon 4/3, 167–204.
BAHNS, J. 1993, Lexical collocations: A contrastive view. *ELT Journal* 47/4, 6–63.
BECKER, A.L. 1991, Language and languaging. *Language & Communication* 11, 33–5.
BEJOINT, H. 1981, The foreign student's use of monolingual English dictionaries: A study of language needs and reference skills. *Applied Linguistics* II/3, 207–22.
BENSON, M., BENSON, E. and ILSON, R. 1986, *The BBI Combinatory Dictionary of English*. Amsterdam/Philadelphia: John Benjamins.
BOGURAEV, B.K. 1991, Building a lexicon: The contribution of computers. *International Journal of Lexicography* Special Issue on Building a Lexicon 4/3, 227–60.
CANDLIN C. 1988, Introduction. In R. CARTER and M. McCARTHY (eds) *Vocabulary and Language Teaching*. London: Longman.

CARTER, R. 1987, Vocabulary and second/foreign language teaching. *Language Teaching* 20, 3–16.
CARTER, R. and McCARTHY, M. (eds) 1988, *Vocabulary and Language Teaching*. London: Longman.
CHANNELL. J. 1981, Applying semantic theory to vocabulary teaching. *English Language Teaching Journal* 35/2, 115–22.
CLEAR, J. 1993, The British National Corpus. In G.P. LANDOW and P. DELANY (eds) *The Digital Word: Text-based Computing in the Humanities* (pp. 163–87). Cambridge, MA: MIT Press.
CORNU, A-M. 1979, The first step in vocabulary teaching. *Modern Language Journal* 63, 262–72.
COSERIU, E. 1975. *Die Geschichte der Sprachphilosophie von der Antike bis zur Gegenwart* 2nd edn. Bd.1. Tübingen.
COWIE, A. 1992, Multiword lexical units and communicative language teaching. In P.J.L. ARNAUD and H.BEJOINT (eds) *Vocabulary and Applied Linguistics* (pp. 1–12). Basingstoke: Macmillan.
COWIE, A.P. 1981, Lexicography and its pedagogic applications: An introduction. *Applied Linguistics* II/3, 203–6.
DE BOT, K., COX, A., RALSTON, S., SCHAUFELI, A. and WELTENS, B. 1995, Lexical processing in bilinguals. *Second Language Research* 11/1, 1–19.
DORNSEIFF, F. 1970, *Der deutsche Wortschatz nach Sachgruppen* 7th edn. Berlin: de Gruyter.
DROSDOWSKI. G. 1988, *Duden Stilwörterbuch der deutschen Sprache*. Mannheim: Duden Verlag.
DUNBAR, G. 1991, *The Cognitive Lexicon*. Tübingen: Gunter Narr.
ESSER, U. and HARNISCH, A. 1980, Eine methodische Variante zur Optimierung des Wortschatzerwerbs: Listen- versus Graphenlernen. *Deutsch als Fremdsprache* 17, 161–6.
FÆRCH, C., HAASTRUP, K. and PHILLIPSON, R. 1984, *Learner Language and Language Learning*. Clevedon: Multilingual Matters.
FOX, J., LABBETT, B., MATTHEWS, C., ROMANO-HVID, C. and SCHOSTAK, J. 1992, *New Perspectives in Modern Language Learning*. A report by the University of East Anglia for the Learning Methods Branch of the Department of Employment.
GASS. S.M. and SELINKER, L. 1994, *Second Language Acquisition*. Hillsdale, NJ: Lawrence Erlbaum.
HALLIG, R. and von WARTBURG, W. 1952, *Begriffssystem als Grundlage für die Lexikographie. Versuch eines Ordnungsschemas*. Berlin: Akademie-Verlag.
HILL, C.P. 1985, Alternatives to dictionaries. In R. ILSON (ed.) *Dictionaries, Lexicography and Language Learning* (pp. 115–21). Oxford: Pergamon Press.
HOLMES-HIGGIN, P. and AHMAD, K. 1992, *The Machine Assisted Terminology Elicitation Environment: Text and Data Processing and Management in Prolog*. Report: CS-92-11. Guildford: University of Surrey, Department of Mathematical & Computing Sciences.
HOLMES-HIGGIN, P., GRIFFIN, S., HOOK, S. and RAZA ABIDI, S. 1993, *User Guide: System Quirk*. Guildford: University of Surrey (ESPRIT 5304, Multilex Report).
HOOK, S. and AHMAD, K. 1992, *Conceptual Graphs and Term Elaboration: Explicating (Terminological) Knowledge*. Guildford: University of Surrey. CS Report No. CS-92-08.

HULSTIJN, J.H. 1994, Die Schlüsselwortmethode: Ein Weg zum Aufbau des Lernerlexikons in der Fremdsprache. In W. BÖRNER and K. VOGEL (eds) *Kognitive Linguistik und Fremdsprachenerwerb. Das mentale Lexikon* (pp. 169–83). Tübingen: Gunter Narr.
ILSON, R. (ed.) 1985, *Dictionaries, Lexicography and Language Learning*. Oxford: Pergamon Press.
JAIN, M.P. 1981, On meaning in the foreign learner's dictionary. *Applied Linguistics* II/3, 274–86.
JOHNSEN, L. and BUHL, O. 1993, *The LSP Student's Workbench*. Paper presented at the 9th Eurpopean Symposium on Language for Special Purposes, Bergen, Norway, 2–6 August 1993.
KIPFER, B. 1987, Dictionaries and the intermediate student: Communicative needs and the development of user reference skills. In A. COWIE (ed.) *The Dictionary and the Language Learner* (pp. 44–54). Tübingen: Max Niemeyer Verlag.
KIRKPATRICK, E. 1987, *Roget's Thesaurus*. London: Longman.
KJELLMER, G. 1994, *A Dictionary of English Collocations*. Oxford: Clarendon Press.
KOHN, K. 1990, Terminological knowledge for translation purposes. In R. ARNTZ and G. THOME (eds) *Übersetzungswissenschaft: Ergebnisse und Perspektiven* (pp. 199–206). Tübingen: Gunter Narr.
KOLLER, W. 1992, *Einführung in die Übersetzungswissenschaft* 4th edn. Heidelberg/Wiesbaden: Quelle and Meyer.
KROLL, J.F. 1993, Accessing conceptual representations for words in a second language. In R. SCHREUDER and B. WELTENS (eds) *The Bilingual Lexicon* (pp. 53–81). Amsterdam/Philadelphia: John Benjamins.
KUGLER, M., AHMAD, K. and THURMAIR, G. (eds) 1995, *Translator's Workbench. Tools and Terminology for Translation and Text Processing*, Research reports ESPRIT, Project 2315. Berlin: Springer-Verlag.
LEVIN, B. 1991, Building a lexicon: The contribution of linguistics. *International Journal of Lexicography* Special Issue on Building a Lexicon 4/3, 205–26.
LYONS, J. 1977, *Semantics* Vol.1. Cambridge: Cambridge University Press.
McARTHUR, T. 1981, *The Longman Lexicon of Contemporary English*. Harlow: Longman.
McCARTHY, M. 1990, *Vocabulary*. Oxford: Oxford University Press.
MEARA, P. 1984, The study of lexis in interlanguage. In A. DAVIES, C. CRIPER, and A.P.R. HOWATT (eds) *Interlanguage* (pp. 225–35). Edinburgh: Edinburgh University Press.
— 1992, Network structures and vocabulary acquisition in a foreign language. In P.J.L. ARNAUD and H. BEJOINT (eds) *Vocabulary and Applied Linguistics* (pp. 62–70). Basingstoke: Macmillan.
— 1993, The bilingual lexicon and the teaching of vocabulary. In R. SCHREUDER and B. WELTENS (eds) *The Bilingual Lexicon* (pp. 279–97). Amsterdam/Philadelphia: John Benjamins.
MEL'CUK, I. 1984, 1988, 1992, *Dictionnaire Explicatif et Combinatoire du Français Contemporain: Recherches Lexico-Sémantiques I, II, III*. Montréal: Les Presses de l'Université de Montréal.
MEL'CUK, I. and ZHOLKOVSKY, A. 1984. *Explanatory Combinatorial Dictionary of Modern Russian*. Vienna: Wiener Slawistischer Almanach.
MILLER, G.A. 1978, Semantic relations among words. In M. HALLE, J. BRESNAN and G.A. MILLER (eds) *Linguistic Theory and Psychological Reality* (pp. 60–118). Cambridge, MA: MIT Press.

MILLER, G.A. and FELLBAUM, C. 1992, WordNet and the organisation of lexical memory. In M.L. SWARTZ and M. YAZDANI (eds) *Intelligent Tutoring Systems for Foreign Language Learning* (pp. 89–102). Berlin: Springer-Verlag.
PICHT, H. and DRASKAU, J. 1985, *Terminology: An Introduction.* Guildford: University of Surrey.
RIVERS, W. 1983, *Speaking in Many Tongues: Essays in Foreign-Language Teaching* 3rd edn. Cambridge: Cambridge University Press.
ROGERS, M. and AHMAD, K. 1990, The learner, learners' errors and ICALL. In M. LJUNG (ed.) *The Use of Computers in Language Teaching and Research.* Proceedings from the Stockholm Conference, September 7–9, 1989, (pp. 93–112). Stockholm: University of Stockholm.
ROSSNER, R. 1985, The learner as lexicographer: Using dictionaries in second language learning. In R. ILSON (ed.) *Dictionaries, Lexicography and Language Learning* (pp. 95–102). Oxford: Pergamon Press.
RUDMAN, M. (ed.) 1993, *Longman Language Activator.* Harlow: Longman.
SAVILLE-TROIKE, M. 1984, What *really* matters in second language learning for academic achievement? *TESOL Quarterly* 18/2, 199–219.
SCHMITT, P.A. 1986, Die Eindeutigkeit von Fachtexten: Bermerkungen zu einer Fiktion. In M. SNELL-HORNBY (ed.) *Übersetzungswissenschaft: eine Neuorientierung* (pp. 250–82). Tübingen: Francke.
SCHREUDER, R. and WELTENS, B. (eds) 1993, *The Bilingual Lexicon.* Amsterdam/Philadelphia: John Benjamins.
SNELL-HORNBY, M. 1993, Word against text: the role of semantics in translation. In G. JÄGER, and K. GOMMLICH (eds) *Text and Meaning* (pp. 105–12). Kent, OH: Kent State University Press.
SNODGRASS, J.G. 1993, Translating *versus* picture naming. Similarities and differences. In R. SCHREUDER and B. WELTENS (eds) *The Bilingual Lexicon* (pp. 83–114). Amsterdam/Philadelphia: John Benjamins.
SUMMERS, D. 1988a, The role of dictionaries in language learning. In R. CARTER. and M. McCARTHY (eds) *Vocabulary and Language Teaching* (pp. 111–23). London: Longman.
— 1988b, English language teaching dictionaries: Past, present and future. *English Today* 4/2, 10–16.
SWARTZ, M.L. 1992, Issues for tutoring knowledge in foreign language intelligent tutoring sytems. In M.L. SWARTZ and M. YAZDANI (eds) *Intelligent Tutoring Systems for Foreign Language Learning* (pp. 219–33). Berlin: Springer-Verlag.
SWARTZ, M.L., KOSTYLA, S.J., HANFLING, S. and HOLLAND, V.M. 1990, Preliminary assessment of a foreign language learning environment. *CALL* 1, 51–64.
TAYLOR, L. 1990, *Teaching and Learning Vocabulary.* New York: Prentice Hall.
TOMASZCZYK, J. 1979, Dictionaries: Users and uses. *Glottodidactica* 12, 103–19.
TRIBBLE, C. and JONES. G. 1990, *Concordances in the Classroom.* Harlow: Longman.
VERHALLEN, M. and SCHOONEN, R. 1993, Lexical knowledge of monolingual and bilingual children. *Applied Linguistics* 14/4, 344–63.
WILLIS, D. 1990, *The Lexical Syllabus.* Glasgow: Collins ELT.
— 1994, A lexical approach. In M. BYGATE, A. TONKYN and E. WILLIAMS (eds) *Grammar and the Language Teacher* (pp. 56–66). New York: Prentice Hall.
ZGUSTA, L. 1971, *Manual of Lexicography.* Prague: Academia/The Hague & Paris: Mouton.

ZOCK, M. 1992, SWIM or sink: the problem of communicating thought. In M.L. SWARTZ and M. YAZDANI (eds) *Intelligent Tutoring Systems for Foreign Language Learning* (pp.235–47). Berlin: Springer-Verlag.

Index

accuracy, and learning methods 29
acquisition, L1
— and prototype theory 41, 42–5
— stages 5, 21–2, 24
— and vocabulary size 16
acquisition, L2
— and advanced learners 38, 75
— by children 5
— and contrastive analysis hypothesis 2
— and dictionaries 80–4
— of English 10–11
— and lexical needs 71–4
— and prototype theory 9–10, 18, 41, 46–8
— research 7–8, 27–39
— and teaching methods 74–80
— and technology 12–13, 69, 70, 71, 84–90
acronyms 11, 65, 67
activation, interactive 23
adjectives, and translation equivalence 57
adults, and underextension 7
adverbs, and translation equivalence 57
affixation, and word formation 66
Ahmad, K. 71
Aitchison, Jean 15–24
— and language acquisition 21–2, 24
— and links between words 7, 19–20, 24, 73
— and prototype theory 17–19, 24, 53
— and vocabulary size 6, 10, 15–16, 24
— and word retrieval 7, 8, 22–4
— and word storage 6, 7, 12–13, 17–19, 24
Albee, Edward 2
Anderman, Gunilla 1–13, 57
— and covert mental models 6, 10
— and prototype theory 9–10, 41–53
Anderson, J. 28, 29, 34

aphasia, and coordinate links 20
Aristotle, and word meaning 17
Austin, J.L. 4
Ayto, John, and neologisms 11–12, 63–8

Bailey, D. 28, 30, 32, 34
Bassnett-McGuire, S. 3
bilingualism, and vocabulary acquisition 73–4
blends 22, 65, 73
Bloom, L.M. 44
Boguraev, B.K. 80–1, 84
Bonham, D.N. 28, 31
borrowing, linguistic 51
Bowerman, M. 43, 44
brain
— computer models 23
— parallel distributed processing model 23
brain damage, and selection errors 20
Broeder, P. et al. 37
Bryson, B. 58

CALL (computer-assisted language learning) 85, 90
categorisation
— by adults 46
— by children 6, 9, 18–19, 21–2, 41, 42–3
— and translation 48
— see also prototypes
Catford, J.C. 1
CD, multimedia 88
CD-ROM 88
change, semantic 11, 65–6
Chapman, I. 28, 30
Chesterman, A. 4
children
— and categorisation 6, 9, 18–19, 21–2, 41–3
— and overextension 7, 21–2, 24, 43

— and underextension 7, 21
— and vocabulary size 16
— and word acquisition 7, 21-2, 24, 41
Chomsky, Noam, and theory-based approach to language 1, 4-5
cognates, in vocabulary learning 8-9, 29, 33, 37, 77
coinage of new words 11, 64-8
communication, interlingual 3
complexity, and word acquisition 43-4
compounding, and word formation 11, 65-6
computer
— and electronic dictionaries 83-4
— and ICALL systems 85-6, 88-90
— in L2 acquisition 12-13, 69, 71, 78, 84-90
— and word formation 12, 67
— *see also* workbench-for-words
concepts
— and bilingual lexical matrix 73-4
— and computer systems 86, 88
— and dictionaries 80-4, 90
— and graph theory 75-6, 78-9, 88
— and subject specialisms 4
context
— and links between words 7, 20, 21
— and macro-context 3
— and word learning 29, 30, 34, 71-2
contrastive analysis 2, 46
coordinates, and word linkage 7, 19-20, 24, 72-3
corpora *see* text
Coseriu, E. 69-70
course design
— and impact of research 36
— for translation studies 8-9
Cruttenden, 37
culture
— and prototypicality 6, 18-19, 24
— and translation equivalence 51-2, 58, 62

Danish, as SL 79
database, in workbench-for-words 88
derivation, and word formation 11, 65
dialect, and social structure 2
dialogue, translation 3
dictionaries

— collocational 82-3
— electronic 83-4, 88
— and learner needs 12-13, 49, 70-2, 74, 79
— as models of lexical knowledge 80-4
— and neologisms 11-12, 63-8
— semantically-based 12-13, 74, 81-4
— and thesauri 81-2
— and translator needs 70
Dornsieff, F. 81

English
— grammar 58-61
— items/systems 37
— L2 learners 11, 77
— and new words 10-12
— as SL 48-9, 50, 58
— as TL 79
— and translation equivalence 10, 56-62
— and vocabulary acquisition 33, 37
— vocabulary size 8, 10-11, 24, 37, 57-60
environment, and neologisms 67-8
equivalence, translation 10, 49, 52
— and collocational patterns 83
— and English as source language 10, 56-62
— perfect 10, 56-7
— and prototypes 41
— and specialist language 69-70, 74
error
— explanation of 2
— lexical/grammatical 70, 72, 85
— prediction of 2
— selection 20, 22
Esser, U. 75-6, 78

Færsch, C. 76
Farrar, F.W. 15-16
Fellbaum, C. 73
fiction, popular, in translation 48-9
field, semantic
— in L1 acquisition 43-4, 72
— in L2 acquisition 47-8, 72-3, 77, 90
— in translation 78-9
Fillmore, C.J. 51
finance, and word formation 12, 67
Fodor, J.A. 15

Foltz, M. 28, 31
foreign language teaching, and contrastive analysis hypothesis 2
Forlano, G. 28, 30, 32
Fox, J. 90
frames, cultural
— in L1 acquisition 51
— in translation 51–2
French, L2 learners 48

Gass, S. 36, 37, 87
Gellerstam, M. 48–50
German
— dictionaries 70, 81, 83
— and L2 learners 47–8
Gilbert, L. 28, 30, 32
Gildea, P.M. 16, 24
grammar
— English 10, 58–61
— scale and category 1
— transformational generative 1
graph theory 75–6, 78–9, 81, 88
Grinstead, W. 28, 29, 31–2, 33, 34, 36
Gutt, E.-A. 3

Haastrup, K. 76
Halliday, Michael 1, 60, 90
Hallig, R. 81–2
Harnisch, A. 76, 78
Heidelberg project 47–8
Hinton, G.E. 23
Hoffman, M. 28, 30, 32

ICALL (intelligent computer-assisted language learning) 85–6, 88–90
interlanguage 76
International Organisation for Standardisation 56–7

Jones, G. 88
Jordan, A. 28, 29, 34

Katz, J.J. 15
Kirkpatrick, E. 81
knowledge, lexical, and dictionaries 80–4
KonText 87
Kopstein, F. 28, 31, 33
Kotsinas, U.-B. 47

Kugler, M. 71

Labov, William 17
Lado, Robert 2
Lakoff, G. 6, 17, 46
language
— connectionist models 23
— learning *see* acquisition
— for special purposes 69–70, 79, 83
— spoken 64
learning, aloud/silent 29
Leopardi, G. 62
Leopold, W.F. 21
lexicogrammar, of English 60
lexicon
— bilingual matrix 73–4
— development 63–8
— and graph theory 75–6, 78–9, 81, 88
— growth of interest in 5, 13, 15, 24, 27, 74
— neglect of 4, 8, 13, 15, 27, 74
— semantic organisation 73–4, 75–80, 81–4, 90
— structure 8, 38, 75
— *see also* vocabulary
lexis, English 60–1
LEXNET-INSITU 75–6
lifestyle, and neologisms 67
linguistics
— contrastive 58
— and translation studies 1–3, 13, 48–53
links
— collocational 7, 20, 24, 72–3, 77–9
— and collocational dictionaries 82–3
— and coordinates 7, 19–20, 24, 72–3
lists, learning words from 8–9, 29–31, 34–5, 76–7
Lively, Penelope 15
loan-words, in English 10
Lyons, J. 82

McArthur, T. 82
McCarthy, M. 77–8
McClelland, J.L. 23
Major, D.R. 42–3
manner, expression 9, 45, 50, 57
map, semantic 77–8
markedness 9, 46, 49
meaning

INDEX
99

— and associative networks 12, 34, 72, 73, 75–6, 78
— changes in 11
— codification 80–4
— denotational 72
— family resemblance theory 17
— as fixed 17
— as fuzzy 6, 17
— learning 28–30, 72
— and prototypes 6, 9, 17–19
Meara, Paul 10, 12
— and cognates 8–9, 29, 33, 37, 77
— and L2 lexicon 70, 73, 75, 81
— and research in L2 7–9, 27–39
metaphor, and covert mental models 6, 10, 19, 53
Microconcord 87
Miller, G.A. 16, 24, 73
mind, brain metaphor 23
Mini Concordancer 87
models, covert 6, 10, 19, 53
models of lexical knowledge, dictionaries as 80–4
Morgan, C. 28, 30–1, 32, 34
morphology, derivational 60
motion verbs
— and L1 acquisition 44–5
— and L2 acquisition 9, 47–8, 50
— and translation 9, 57

neologisms
— and coinage 11, 64–6
— and dictionaries 11–12, 63–8
— in English 10–12
— sources 12, 64–6, 67–8
— survival 11, 64, 66–7
networks
— associative 12, 34, 72, 73, 75–6, 78–9, 84, 85, 90
— propositional 85
Neubert, A. 51–2
Newmark, Peter, and translation into English 8, 10–11, 56–62
Nida, E.A. 1, 3–4, 50
nouns
— phrasal 61
— and translation equivalence 57

overextension

— and L1 acquisition 7, 21–2, 24, 43
— and L2 acquisition 47–8
particles, in Swedish 49
Phillipson, R. 76
pragmatics, cross-cultural 2–3
prepositions, in English 60
prototypes
— and covert mental models 6, 10, 19, 53
— hierarchies 6, 24
— and L1 acquisition 41, 42–5
— and L2 acquisition 9–10, 18, 41, 46–8, 50
— in learning meanings 6, 9, 17–19
— and overextension 22, 24, 47
— and translation 6, 10, 18, 48–53

recall, testing 29–30, 75–6
recall method, in word learning 29
register
— in English 10, 57, 61
— and L2 acquisition 48–9
relearning, research on 29
relevance theory 3
repetition, in word learning 29
research, L1 acquisition 41–5
research, L2 acquisition 7–8, 27–39
— and advanced learners 38, 75
— assessment 35, 38–9
— and individual differences 8, 31–2, 36, 37
— learning methods 34–5
— number of subjects 31–2, 36, 37
— number of target words 33–4
— and prototype theory 46–8
— range of target languages 32–3, 37
— standardisation 38–9
— themes 28–31
research, translation, and prototype theory 41, 48
Richards, J. 38
Rivers, W. 90
Rogers, Margaret 1–13
— and technology in L2 acquisition 12–13, 69–90
Roget, P.M. 81, 82
Romance languages, and translation into English 9, 11, 45, 50
Roshal, S. 28, 31, 33

Rossner, R. 72
Rumelhart, D.E. 23

Schlesinger, I.M. 51
science, translation as 1, 3
Seibert, L. 28, 29, 30, 32
Selincker, L. 87
semantics
— change 11, 65–6
— and organisation of lexicon 73–80, 81–4, 90
— semantic map 77–8
— *see also* field, semantic
Shakespeare, William, vocabulary size 16
shape, and infant categorisation 43
Shreve, G.M. 51
skills, vocabulary, individual differences in 8, 31–2, 36
Snell-Hornby, M. 3, 52
sociolinguistics, and translation 2
source language
— and dialect 2
— explicit expression of 50–1
Spanish, as TL 50
speech acts, and cross-cultural pragmatics 2–3
Sperber, 3
Stoddard, G. 28, 30, 32, 35
Sully, James 21
Summers, D. 71
Swartz, M.L. 85
Swedish
— and L2 learners 47
— as TL 48–9
SWIM (See What I Mean) system 86
synonyms
— dictionary coverage 70, 72, 84
— in English 11, 61
syntax
— interest in 4, 13, 15
— and language universals 5
System Quirk 87, 88

Taber, C.R. 50
target language
— and acquisition research 32–3, 37
— and dialect 2
Taylor, L. 77

teaching methods, L2 24, 49–50, 71
— lexically-based 75–80
— and technology 84–90
technology, and L2 acquisition 12–13, 69, 71, 84–90
terminology
— concept-based 78
— translation-oriented 70
text
— and context 3
— as learning resource 79, 87–8
— and word 4
textbooks, and selection of prototypes 18
thesauri 81–2
Thorndike, E. 28, 29
Thurmair, G. 71
translation
— computer-assisted 69
— course design 8–9
— and mental lexicon size 6
— of popular fiction 48–9
— and prototype theory 6, 10, 18, 48–53
— sense-for-sense 4
— technical 56–7, 69–70, 71, 78, 80
— as technology 3–4
— text-for-text 4
— word-for-word 4, 73–4, 76
translation studies
— and linguistics 1–3, 13, 48–53
— multidisciplinary approach 3–4
— and prototypology 41–2
— and teaching methods 8–9
translation theory, and contrastive linguistics 58
'translationese' 9, 48–50
Tribble, C. 88

underextension 7, 21, 24
universals
— and mental models 53
— and syntax 5
use of language, and L2 learners 71

verbs
— and collocational links 20
— in English 10
— L1 acquisition 43–5
— L2 acquisition 46–8, 50
— modal 60

INDEX

— of motion *see* motion verbs
— nuclear 9, 46–8, 49
— phrasal 60–1
— plus *-ing* 10, 59–60
— and translation equivalence 57
Viberg, Å. 47
vocabulary
— acquisition 7–8, 27–39, 70, 72–3
— interlanguage 76
— latent 77
— learner needs 71–4
— lists 8–9, 29–31, 34–5, 49, 76–7
— size 6, 10–11, 15–16, 24, 37, 57–60
— specialised 69–70, 71
— teaching 49–50, 71, 74–80, 84–90
— *see also* lexicon

Wartburg, W. von 81–2
Waugh, Evelyn 17
Williams, Tennessee 2
Wilson, 3
Wittgenstein, Ludwig, and family resemblance theory of meaning 17
word
— designative 72–3
— paradigmatic relations 4, 72
— semantic relations 73–4, 75–80, 81–4, 90

— syntagmatic relations 4, 72
— and text 4
word formation 10–12, 63–8
— sources 12, 64–6, 67–8
— survival rate 11, 64, 66–7
word frequency
— and nuclear verbs 46–8
— in target text 9, 48–9
word retrieval 7, 8, 22–4, 73–4, 76
— interactive activation model 23, 24
— and workbench-for-words 88
word storage 12–13, 17–19, 72–3
— and links between words 7, 19–20, 24, 72–4, 77–9
— and prototypes 6, 17–19, 24
— thesaurus-based 12–13
— and workbench-for-words 88
WordNet system 84
workbench-for-words
— and electronic dictionaries 88
— and L2 learning 12–13, 86–90
— and text-processing tools 87–8
— and translation 71, 78, 79
— and vocabulary storage and retrieval 88

Zgusta, L. 80

For Product Safety Concerns and Information please contact our EU Authorised Representative:

Easy Access System Europe

Mustamäe tee 50

10621 Tallinn

Estonia

gpsr.requests@easproject.com

www.ingramcontent.com/pod-product-compliance
Lightning Source LLC
Chambersburg PA
CBHW022016300426
44117CB00005B/218